INDIANA WILDLIFE VIEWING GUIDE

Phil T. Seng and David J. Case

FALCON PRESS ®

ACKNOWLEDGMENTS

STEERING COMMITTEE

The following individuals provided invaluable guidance throughout this project. Their experience and expertise was particularly helpful concerning the selection of wildlife viewing sites and educational concepts, planning the location and placement of highway signs, and editing materials for the guide.

Jack Arnold, National Park Service
Alice Bentley, South Bend Audubon Society
Jim Bergens, Indiana Chapter, The Wildlife Society
Nadine Bonds, GTE
Christine Combs, Northern Indiana Public Service Company
Marge Filchak, Association of Indiana Convention and Visitors Bureaus
Vince Griffin, PSI Energy
Gene Hopkins, Indiana Bowhunters Association
Dave Hudak, U.S. Fish and Wildlife Service
Sheila Hughes, The Nature Conservancy
Indiana Department of Natural Resources:
    Glenn Lange, Division of Fish and Wildlife
    Steve Locke, Division of State Parks
    Jim Gerbracht, Division of Reservoir Management
    John Bacone, Division of Nature Preserves
    Dan Henkel, Division of Public Information and Education
    Keely Phelps, Division of Outdoor Recreation
    Ben Hubbard, Division of Forestry
Larry Mullins, U.S. Forest Service
Harry Nikides, Indiana Wildlife Federation
Marcia Peters and Frank Vukovits, Indiana Department of Transportation
Peggy Rutledge and Florence Fleck, Indiana Department of Commerce

In addition to those mentioned above, the following people contributed significantly to the completion of this project:

Patrick R. Ralston, Director of the Indiana Department of Natural Resources and Edward L. Hansen, former Chief of the Indiana Department of Natural Resources, Fish and Wildlife Division, for their foresight and support in getting this project off the ground.

Jennifer Huggins and Melissa Nelson, D.J. Case & Associates, for researching and tracing the viewing site maps, and for providing administrative support throughout the project.

Steven Barr, for developing and creating the artistic concepts found in the guide.

Front Cover Photo: White-tailed buck in velvet, MARK PICARD
Back Cover Photos: Pileated woodpecker, SCOTT NIELSEN
Turkey Run State Park, MARK ROMESSER

"There are some who can live without wild things, and some who cannot."

-Aldo Leopold, A Sand County Almanac

This guide is dedicated to those who cannot.

Author
Phil T. Seng

Project Managers
David J. Case and Phil T. Seng
D.J. Case & Associates

CONTENTS

REGION TWO: CROSSROADS

REGION THREE: HILL COUNTRY

White-tailed deer fawns have white spots on their coats that help conceal them while hiding. The spots imitate the partial sunlight that filters through the trees onto the brown forest floor. BRENT PARRETT

PROJECT SPONSORS

Major financial and logistical support for this project was provided by the following organizations:

The U.S. FOREST SERVICE is responsible for the management of National Forest lands and their resources. As stewards of these lands, the Forest Service protects, restores, and manages them to provide various values to best serve the needs of the American people. The Hoosier National Forest in southern Indiana is a sponsor of this program to promote awareness and enjoyment of fish and wildlife on public lands. Hoosier National Forest, 811 Constitution Avenue, Bedford, IN 47421. (812) 275-5987.

The INDIANA DEPARTMENT OF NATURAL RESOURCES, DIVISION OF FISH AND WILDLIFE has the responsibility to properly manage the state's fish and wildlife resources for the use and enjoyment of the people of Indiana. Management is based on the most up-to-date technical information available and human aspects receive constant attention. Proper management implies maintaining population levels in harmony with ecological, social, and economic values of the human community. Habitat management activities on fish and wildlife areas are funded through hunting and fishing license revenue and federal aid funds from the Wildlife and Sport Fish Restoration Programs. The federal funds are derived from excise taxes on firearms, ammunition, and fishing tackle. 402 West Washington, Rm. W273, Indianapolis, IN 46204. (317) 232-4080.

THE U.S. FISH AND WILDLIFE SERVICE is pleased to support this project in furtherance of its mission to conserve, protect, and enhance fish and wildlife resources and their habitats. In Indiana, the Service manages the Muscatatuck and Patoka River national wildlife refuges, and is active in wetland and other habitat protection and restoration, contaminant cleanup, and enforcement of federal fish and wildlife laws. 718 N. Walnut St., Bloomington, IN 47401. (812) 334-4261.

THE NATIONAL FISH AND WILDLIFE FOUNDATION, chartered by Congress to stimulate private giving to conservation, is an independent not-for-profit organization. Using federally funded challenge grants, it forges partnerships between public and private sectors to conserve the nation's fish, wildlife, and plants. National Fish and Wildlife Foundation, 18th and C Street N.W., Washington DC 20240. (202) 208-4051.

The INDIANA WILDLIFE FEDERATION (IWF) is a statewide, non-governmental, non-profit conservation education organization governed by a volunteer Board of Directors. IWF is an association of individuals and local affiliate groups with the basic objectives to promote environmental education and wise management of Indiana's natural resources. A one-year membership is $15.00 and includes six issues of the bi-monthly magazine, *Hoosier Conservation*. To join or for more information write or call Indiana Wildlife Federation, 301 E. Carmel Drive, Suite G-200, Carmel, IN 46032. (317) 571-1220.

DEFENDERS OF WILDLIFE is a national, nonprofit organization of more than 80,000 members and supporters dedicated to preserving the natural abundance and diversity of wildlife and its habitat. A one-year membership is $20 and includes six issues of the bimonthly magazine, *Defenders*. To join or for further information, write or call Defenders of Wildlife, 1244 Nineteenth Street N.W., Washington, DC 20036. (202) 659-9510.

 GTE is a world leader in its three core businesses—telecommunications, lighting, and precision materials. GTE subsidiaries, operating in 48 states and 41 countries, include the largest U.S.-based local telephone company. GTE North Telephone Operations headquarters is located in Westfield, Indiana. GTE North has approximately 19,000 employees accounting for nearly $730 million in total wages and salaries. In 1990, GTE North produced revenues of $2.2 million. It serves 2.9 million access lines in nearly 4,000 communities. In 1990, GTE North contributed nearly $2.6 million to various charitable and community service organizations in its ten-state operating area consisting of Illinois, Indiana, Maine, Michigan, New Hampshire, New York, Ohio, Pennsylvania, Vermont, and Wisconsin. GTE North Corporate Headquarters, P.O. Box 407, Westfield, IN. (317) 896-6464.

 NORTHERN INDIANA PUBLIC SERVICE COMPANY is the state's largest gas and electric utility, and is dedicated to providing quality products and services and contributing to the quality of life in the communities we serve across northern Indiana. NIPSCO is proud to support this guide as a continuation of our commitment to the preservation of the state's wildlife and environment. (219) 853-5200.

PSIEnergy PSI ENERGY is an energy services company providing power to some 600,000 customers in Indiana. In 1990, PSI dedicated 160 acres at its Gibson Generating Station, located near Princeton, Indiana, as a wet-land habitat for plants and wildlife. The habitat is open to the public. PSI Energy, 1000 East Main Street, Plainfield, IN 46168. (317) 839-9611.

 THE INDIANA DEPARTMENT OF TRANSPORTATION (INDOT) is responsible for the planning, construction, and maintenance of a safe, modern transportation system. All phases of state and interstate highway development are administered by the agency that is headed by Commissioner John J. Dillon. Federal funding for aeronautics, railroads, and public transportation are channelled through INDOT's Office of Intermodal Transportation and Planning. INDOT's Division of Local Assistance also channels federal assistance to local communities and their road projects. The 1991-1992 Indiana State Highway Map may be requested by contacting INDOT at 100 North Senate Avenue, Room N775, Indianapolis, IN 46204, Attention: Map Requests or by calling (317) 232-5115.

 THE INDIANA DEPARTMENT OF COMMERCE, TOURISM AND MARKETING DEVELOPMENT DIVISION promotes the unique attractions, special events, and recreational opportunities of the state. Tourism Development includes heritage tourism pilot programs, rural tourism, sports, and recreation, and education development. The division markets the state through brochure distribution, print/

electronic media, and cooperative advertising. To receive travel packets and general information, contact the division at One North Capitol, Suite 700, Indianapolis, IN 46204 or call (317) 232-8860.

CONTRIBUTORS

Additional financial support for this project was provided by the following organizations:

South Bend Audubon Society
Amos Butler Chapter, The Audubon Society
Indiana Chapter, The Wildlife Society
Association of Indiana Convention and Visitors Bureaus

Welcome to Indiana's great outdoors!

Indiana has been blessed with a variety and abundance of scenic natural areas, but many people are unaware of the tremendous natural beauty to be found here. Unique sand dunes ecosystems occur along our portion of Lake Michigan; natural lakes left behind by glaciers dot our northeast corner; rugged, forested hills and extensive limestone cave systems cover our southcentral region; and numerous sloughs and backwaters of the Ohio River line our southern border. Within these unique habitats and ecosystems live a host of beautiful, unusual, and fascinating animals—Indiana's wildlife. We'd like you to share these wonderful natural resources with us.

This *Indiana Wildlife Viewing Guide* contains eighty-nine sites, highlighting wildlife and natural resources around the state. It tells you how and where to see wildlife, provides a wealth of information about wildlife and the habitats on which they depend, and even keeps you smiling with interesting and often amusing facts about the animals that call Indiana home.

Regardless of where you live or travel in Indiana, there are sites in this guide near you—many of which you may not even realize are there! Take the Guide with you and visit some of these areas soon.

This Guide was developed through a partnership of federal and state agencies, nonprofit conservation organizations, and private corporations. On behalf of all of these cooperators, let us point the way toward the nearest site and bid you "good viewing!"

Sincerely,   Evan Bayh   Frank O'Bannon

Governor   Lieutenant Governor

INTRODUCTION: WILDLIFE VIEWING IN INDIANA

If you're interested in watching wildlife, you'll find that Indiana has a lot to offer. When settlers arrived here, the northern half of the state was covered with prairie, wetlands, and pothole lakes, while the southern half consisted of nearly unbroken hardwood forest. Although the face of the land has changed dramatically since then, many people are not aware of the unique and diverse mix of habitats found here—sand dunes along Lake Michigan, glacial lakes, wetlands, limestone cave systems, extensive hardwood forests, and the Wabash and Ohio River corridors. These diverse habitat types provide homes for nearly 700 different kinds of wildlife.

This guide identifies eighty-nine sites in Indiana that offer unique or exceptional opportunities to view native, free-roaming wildlife. It also encourages you to explore these sites and to find other wildlife viewing areas of your own. At some of the sites in this guide you will see wildlife without even leaving your car—but get out anyway if you are able. By stomping through forests and fields, smelling fresh air, and feeling the good earth beneath your feet, you may gain a greater understanding and appreciation of wild things and their homes.

Many sites in this guide have nature centers where you can get brochures and other interpretive materials. This information can make your wildlife viewing experience much more interesting and personal.

So get out and enjoy Indiana's wildlife, and take some friends along too. Seeing wildlife in thier natural habitats and learning about the roles they play in the ecosystem, gives everyone a more personal stake in conserving wildlife and protecting the natural world.

The wildlife and habitats found in Indiana are magnificent and diverse, but they are only a strand in the complex web of life which makes up the earth's ecosystem. Biological diversity, or *biodiversity,* refers to all of the earth's life forms and the ecological functions they perform. The conservation of biodiversity—which is necessary to maintain the health of the planet—requires an understanding of the processes and concepts which link all life together.

Throughout this guide, you will find short educational sections on biodiversity. Some explain biodiversity concepts, like the summary on page 79 which talks about food webs and the ways in which all living things are interrelated. Other summaries describe some of the unique ecosystems found in Indiana, such as wetlands, forests, and prairies.

VIEWING HINTS

Seeing a wild animal in its native habitat is a rewarding experience. Nearly all of Indiana's natural areas offer excellent opportunities to see some kind of wildlife—all you have to do is get out and look. Much of the excitement of wildlife viewing stems from the fact that you can never be sure what you may see. Although some days are better than others, there are several things you can do in preparation for a trip to greatly increase your odds of seeing wildlife.

Move slowly and quietly There probably is nothing you can do to better improve your odds of seeing wildlife than to slow down. Few animals walk with the steady, rhythmic gait that we humans prefer. Try to break the pattern. Take a few stealthy steps; then stop, look, and listen. Walk into the wind whenever possible.

Watch in the early morning and late evening Generally, there is more wildlife activity in the first and last hours of daylight than any other time of day. The low-angle sunlight of morning and evening also provides rich, warm colors that make beautiful photographs.

Learn about your quarry You will greatly increase your chances if you learn a little about how that animal "makes a living." For instance, chipmunks and woodchucks are highly visible in the fall, because they spend a lot of time feeding to prepare for their winter hibernation.

Choose your season Some wildlife can be seen in Indiana only during certain seasons. Many birds and some insects migrate south during the cold winter months; certain small mammals hibernate; and reptiles and amphibians become dormant and spend the winter underground. Obviously, you will not see any of these animals during the winter. In spring and early summer, however, activity is high, as large numbers of migratory birds return to the state, and most wildlife spend a lot of time eating to make up for the cold, lean winter months.

Use a blind Most wildlife fear humans, and anything you can do to conceal yourself will increase your chances of having a successful viewing experience. This can be as simple as standing behind a tree or bush instead of out in the open. Dark-colored clothes or camouflage may also help. Surprisingly, cars and boats often make excellent viewing blinds. Animals become accustomed to seeing these vehicles, and may not feel threatened or disturbed unless you try to get out.

Use binoculars A pair of binoculars can open up a whole new world of wildlife viewing. High-powered binoculars and spotting scopes can be particularly helpful in open country, but are heavy and cumbersome to pack around if you plan to do much hiking.

A survey conducted by the U.S. Fish and Wildlife Service in 1985 found that 84% of Indiana residents enjoyed viewing, feeding, photographing, or studying wildlife. Why not join them? PHIL T. SENG

11

Use field guides These handy little books can add greatly to the wildlife viewing experience. They tell you what habitats an animal prefers, when it is active, what it eats, and other interesting information. There are field guides available that contain nearly every kind of animal and plant found in Indiana.

Be patient That old adage "patience is a virtue" is especially true in wildlife watching. If you arrive at a wildlife viewing site expecting to see a lot of animals right away, you likely will be disappointed. There are sites that offer this kind of experience, at least during certain seasons, but they are the exception rather than the rule. Wild animals have no meetings to attend or appointments to keep. If they detect something unfamiliar while going about their daily routines, they may literally stand motionless for hours. They have all the time in the world, and you will be much more successful in your viewing efforts if you proceed under the same principle.

SAFE WILDLIFE VIEWING

Most people who venture outdoors to view wildlife share a genuine concern for animals and the natural areas in which they live. Unfortunately, even the innocent act of observing can be disastrous to wildlife if it is not done properly. Remembering and practicing the following tips will ensure a safe and healthy experience for you, for the other people who share your interest, and most importantly, for the animals you're watching.

Don't disturb the animals The goal of successful wildlife viewing should be to see animals without interrupting their normal behavior. Under certain conditions, a single disturbance may cause animals to abandon their efforts to breed, abandon eggs in a nest or young in a den, injure themselves while trying to flee, or quit feeding at a time of critical energy need. It is a natural urge to get as close as possible to wildlife, but those few extra steps may actually lead directly to an animal's death. Remember, with a pair of binoculars you can get eight or ten times closer to wildlife without moving a single step.

Never chase or harass animals Chasing or harassing animals can force them to expend valuable energy they need to survive. Animals live on an "energy budget." If forced to "spend" more energy than they "earn," they must break down fat and other body tissues to repay the difference. If they spend more than they earn too often, starvation results.

Don't feed the animals Having a deer eat food from your hand may seem exciting at the time, but consider these facts:
• Animals quickly become dependent on human handouts, and when this extra food source disappears, many may be faced with starvation.
• Animals dependent on human food may approach cars, making them more likely to be hit on the roads.
• Animals accustomed to human foods are more likely to ingest plastic wrappers and other litter that may seriously harm their digestive systems.
• Some animals accustomed to human handouts may actually become aggressive with visitors who refuse to feed them. This situation may lead to human injury, which in turn usually leads to the death of the offending animal.
• Backyard feeders are the exception to the rule. Rember: if you start using a feeder in fall or winter, don't stop until spring.

Don't pick up orphaned or sick animals Wild animals rarely abandon their young. Unfortunately, well-meaning people have often removed young animals from the wild in an effort to "save" them, when the parents of the young were actually waiting in the shadows to carry them back to the nest.

Respect the rights of others Be considerate when approaching wildlife that are already being viewed by other people. Moving too quickly or loudly may spoil the experience for everyone.

Expect insect pests When viewing wildlife during the summer, be prepared for insects. Mosquitoes, horseflies, and ticks are common in Indiana, and all of them will try to get a piece of you if they are able. In particular, check for the tiny deer tick which is capable of carrying Lyme's disease.

HOW TO USE THIS GUIDE

This Guide contains three sections, one for each viewing region in the state. These regions are color-coded with color strips along the pages of each section. Wildlife viewing site locations are listed on the highway map at the beginning of each region. Sites are numbered consecutively from 1 to 89, beginning on the shores of Lake Michigan in the northwest corner of the state.

Each site contains the following elements to help describe and interpret what may be seen.

Wildlife symbols: These symbols show the types of animals and plants that are most likely to be seen on the site or are unique to the area. They do not include all the species that may occur at a site.

Description: Brief account of the site's physical character—what it looks like (rolling hills, dense forest, river floodplain, etc.).

Viewing information: Describes the site's featured wildlife, when and where to look for them, and the relative probability of seeing them (high, moderate, limited, rare). This section may also contain interesting facts about wildlife found at the site. *IMPORTANT NOTES CONCERNING SITE RESTRICTIONS, SAFETY, AND VIEWING CONDITIONS ARE NOTED IN CAPITAL LETTERS.*

Directions: A small map is provided for each site. Short, written directions may also be included for use with the map.

Ownership: Provides the name of the agency or organization that owns or manages the site. Private sites have been included in this book only with the landowner's permission. Please respect their rights when visiting these sites.

The **telephone number** listed after ownership is the number to call if you have questions or comments concerning a specific site. This is usually the number of the site manager.

Recreation symbols: These indicate some of the facilities and opportunities available at each site. The managing agency or organization can provide more information on these and other types of opportunities available.

FEATURED WILDLIFE

 Songbirds

 Upland Birds

 Waterfowl

 Wading Birds

 Shorebirds

 Marine Birds

 Birds of Prey

 Small Mammals

 Hoofed Mammals

 Carnivores

 Freshwater Mammals

 Fish

 Reptiles/ Amphibians

 Insects

 Wildflowers

FACILITIES AND RECREATION

 Parking

 Restrooms

 Picnic

 Trails

 Handicap Accessible

 Small Boats

 Restaurant

 Boat Ramp

 Camping

 Lodging

 Entry Fee

 Bicycling

 Cross-Country Skiing

BEST VIEWING SEASONS

Spring

Summer

Fall

Winter

All Seasons

SITE OWNER/MANAGER ABBREVIATIONS

A single abbreviation is used throughout this guide:
Indiana DNR—Indiana Department of Natural Resources

HIGHWAY SIGNS

As you travel across Indiana, look for this binoculars logo on highway signs. These signs identify wildlife viewing sites throughout the state, including sites not listed in this guide.

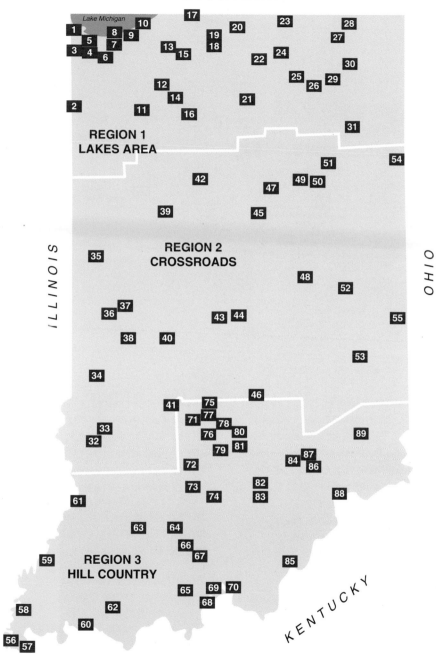

MAP INFORMATION

Indiana's wildlife viewing sites have been organized into the three viewing regions shown on this map. The site descriptions in this guide have been organized by region as well. Each viewing region begins with a detailed map showing the major roads and cities in the region, as well as the location of each wildlife viewing site.

REGION 1 - LAKES AREA

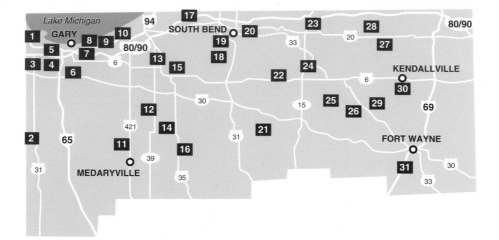

SITE 1 MIGRANT TRAP

SITE 2 LASALLE FISH AND WILDLIFE AREA

SITE 3 HOOSIER PRAIRIE NATURE PRESERVE

SITE 4 OAK RIDGE PRAIRIE COUNTY PARK

SITE 5 GIBSON WOODS NATURE PRESERVE

SITE 6 DEEP RIVER COUNTY PARK

SITE 7 IMAGINATION GLEN PARK

SITE 8 INDIANA DUNES STATE PARK

SITE 9 INDIANA DUNES NATIONAL LAKESHORE

SITE 10 MOUNT BALDY

SITE 11 JASPER-PULASKI FISH AND WILDLIFE AREA

SITE 12 KANKAKEE RIVER FISH AND WILDLIFE AREA

SITE 13 LUHR COUNTY PARK

SITE 14 ROUND LAKE NATURE PRESERVE

SITE 15 KINGSBURY FISH AND WILDLIFE AREA

SITE 16 TIPPECANOE RIVER STATE PARK

SITE 17 SPICER LAKE NATURE PRESERVE

SITE 18 POTATO CREEK STATE PARK

SITE 19 RUM VILLAGE WOODS

SITE 20 MISHAWAKA FISH LADDER

SITE 21 POTAWATOMI WILDLIFE PARK

SITE 22 NAPPANEE ENVIRONMENTAL EDUCATION AREA

SITE 23 BONNEYVILLE MILL COUNTY PARK

SITE 24 RIVER PRESERVE COUNTY PARK

SITE 25 TRI-COUNTY FISH AND WILDLIFE AREA

SITE 26 MERRY LEA ENVIRONMENTAL CENTER

SITE 27 PIGEON RIVER FISH AND WILDLIFE AREA

SITE 28 MAPLEWOOD NATURE CENTER

SITE 29 CHAIN O'LAKES STATE PARK

SITE 30 BIXLER LAKE PARK WETLAND NATURE AREA

SITE 31 FOX ISLAND COUNTY PARK

1 | MIGRANT TRAP

Description: One of the best places in the state to view migrating songbirds in the spring and fall. Small strip of dense, second-growth cottonwood trees on the shore of Lake Michigan. This site is one of the few remaining green spaces in the heart of a heavily industrialized section of Lake Michigan's shoreline. Many birds stop and rest here as they journey around the lake on their spring and fall migrations. For more information on animal migrations, see page 28.

Viewing information: High probability of viewing a great abundance and variety of songbirds and shorebirds in April-May and in August-October. Unusual birds seen here include Connecticut warblers, LeConte's sparrows, and Harris' sparrow. No facilities.

Directions: *From the Indiana Toll Road, take the Calumet Avenue exit. Drive north on Calumet to the Hammond Marina. Turn left into the visitor parking lot. Site is directly west of the marina. A change in ownership and parking arrangements may occur in 1992. Call ahead for details.*

Ownership: Northern Indiana Public Service Company (219) 647-6201
Size: 16 acres   **Closest town:** Hammond

The indigo bunting is not really indigo (deep blue) at all— the female is brown and the male is black. It is the diffraction of sunlight through the male's black feathers that creates this attractive blue sheen.
TOM ULRICH

Gulls play an important role as scavengers, eating whatever fish, freshwater clams, and other dead animals they find washed onto the lakeshore. Occasionally they carry live clams into the air and drop them on rocks to crack them open.

2 | LASALLE FISH AND WILDLIFE AREA

Description: This area is part of the Grand Kankakee Marsh which once covered most of northwest Indiana. The Kankakee River bisects the property, and many small oxbow bayous that once were part of the meandering river channel provide excellent habitat for wetland wildlife. For more information about wetlands, see page 72.

Viewing information: Excellent opportunity to view ducks, geese, herons, egrets, frogs, turtles, snakes, and other wetland wildlife, especially in the waterfowl resting area near parking lot number three. Viewing is best in spring and summer. *THIS IS A PUBLIC HUNTING AREA. WALKING ACCESS IS RESTRICTED FROM OCTOBER THROUGH JANUARY.* Pick up a site map and rules/regulations from the property headquarters.

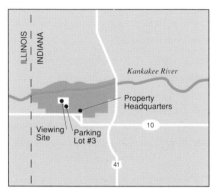

Ownership: Indiana DNR (219) 992-3019
Size: 3,648 acres
Closest town: Lake Village

The green heron may be seen hunting fish, frogs, and other prey in most of Indiana's wetland areas. This crow-sized bird, like many other wildlife species, depends on unpolluted wetland habitats for survival. JOHN SHAW

HOOSIER PRAIRIE NATURE PRESERVE

Description: Large remnant of the prairie landscape that once covered much of northwest Indiana and the Midwest. The area has a great diversity of unique plant and animal life due to the mixture of habitats—tallgrass prairie; wet, marshy areas; and dry, oak-savannah uplands. For more information about prairies, see the next page.

Viewing information: Prairie wildflowers and plants are the primary attraction of this area. The best time to view wildflowers is June through September. Moderate probability of seeing yellowthroat warblers, swamp sparrows, and song sparrows during spring and summer. One-mile trail starts at the parking lot and winds through a portion of the prairie. An excellent brochure describing the sites along the trail is available near the parking lot. Like the prairie landscape prior to settlement, the area is periodically burned. Notice the charred logs from the most recent fire.

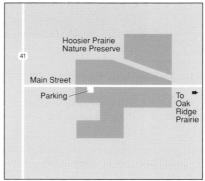

Directions: *From Hammond, travel south on U.S. 41 seven miles to Main Street in Griffith. Turn east on Main Street and proceed .75 mile to the parking lot. From the parking lot, continue east on Main street approximately one mile to the Oak Ridge Prairie viewing site.*

Ownership: Indiana DNR (317) 232-4052
Size: 439 acres   **Closest town:** Griffith

Many unique grasses and wildflowers thrive in the Hoosier Prairie Nature Preserve.

MARK ROMESSER

PRAIRIE: WHERE THE BUFFALO ROAMED

Prior to settlement, great herds of bison roamed the vast expanses of prairie grassland, which covered the central United States from northwest Indiana to the Rocky Mountains. Prairies contain a diverse mixture of unique plants and animals that are specially adapted for life in this environment—many of them cannot be found anywhere else.

Most prairie plants have large underground root systems, some extending more than fifteen feet below the surface. These deep roots play a vital role in the plants' survival by:

- Providing water during periods of drought
- Protecting against soil erosion caused by wind and water
- Choking out invading plants

Perhaps the greatest advantage of these large root systems is their ability to store energy and nutrients so the plants can respond quickly to the natural force which sustains the prairie ecosystem—fire.

Periodic fires are a natural part of the native prairie ecosystem. Over time, prairies are invaded by woody plants and trees, which begin to replace the native prairie plants. However, fires occasionally burn the prairie, consuming nearly everything above the ground. Most of the shallow-rooted invading plants are killed by the intense heat, but the deep roots of the prairie plants are unaffected. Within days, new green shoots appear, and the prairie is renewed.

The majority of America's prairies are gone because the fires that sustain them have been suppressed by people, and because prairie soil makes excellent farmland. It is important that remaining prairielands be protected so the unique assemblage of plants and animals that live here can be enjoyed by future generations.

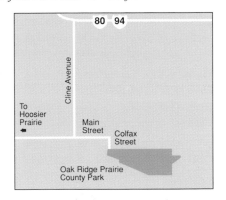

Description: Hiking trails and ski trails provide wildlife viewing along ponds, wetlands, prairie, old fields, and bottomland hardwood forest.

Viewing information: Moderate to high probability of viewing many different songbird species, including indigo bunting, northern oriole, and sedge wren. Muskrats and raccoons are often seen in the wetland areas, and mice, rabbits, and squirrels are common throughout the park. It is possible to see coyotes, red foxes, and mink hunting for these abundant small mammals, especially on summer evenings. The small mammals also attract predators such as red-tailed hawks, northern harriers, screech owls, saw-whet owls, and great-horned owls. Trails through the low areas may flood in spring and fall. Seasonal entry fee required.

Directions: *Exit I-80/94 at Cline Avenue. Travel south four miles to Main Street. Turn east on Main and proceed one mile to Colfax. Turn south on Colfax and drive .25 mile to park entrance. Follow main road to the large parking area. Primary trailhead is located next to the pond behind the Multipurpose Building. Travel west on Main Street approximately one mile to the Hoosier Prairie viewing site.*

Ownership: Lake County Parks & Recreation Dept. (219) 755-3685 or 769-7275
Size: 695 acres
Closest town: Griffith/Merrillville

The muskrat is very common in wetland habitats throughout Indiana. It can remain underwater for more than fifteen minutes, and can swim forward or backward with ease, using its thin, flattened tail as a rudder.

C.D. GRONDAHL

5 GIBSON WOODS NATURE PRESERVE

Description: Long, narrow strip of wooded sand dunes and small wetlands called swales. This area is part of the extensive sand dune ecosystem created by the wind and waves along the south shore of Lake Michigan. For more information about dunes, see page 25.

Viewing information: High probability of viewing warblers, thrushes, and other songbirds, especially in the spring and fall. Gray foxes are fairly common in the area, and a careful observer may be able to see one at dawn or dusk. Limited probability of viewing mink and weasels in the wetland areas and the endangered Franklin's ground squirrel along sandy ridges. Several interesting insects are found here, including the rare Karner blue butterfly and the ant lion. Ant lion larvae build small pit traps in the sand to catch ants and other small insects. Visit the Environmental Awareness Center to pick up interpretive materials and a map of the self-guided nature trail. A wheelchair-accessible boardwalk is available.

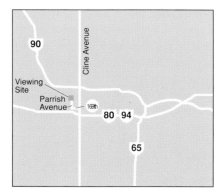

Ownership: Lake County Parks & Recreation Dept. (219) 844-3188 or 755-3685
Size: 130 acres
Closest town: Hammond/Gary

Gray fox kits can hunt for themselves at only four months of age. The gray fox is the only dog-like animal in North America that can truly climb trees. R.E. BARBER

6 DEEP RIVER COUNTY PARK

Description: Hiking trails follow the meandering course of Deep River. River floodplain and gentle to steep slopes with hardwood forest.

Viewing information: High probability of viewing wading birds such as great blue herons, green herons, and American bitterns in summer and fall. Excellent viewing of spring warbler migrations and other woodland songbirds throughout the year. An observation deck provides a vista of the river. Inquire at the visitor center about the location of this vista; it is not identified on the trail map.

Ownership: Lake County Parks & Recreation Dept. (219) 769-9030 or 755-3685
Size: 1,000 acres
Closest town: Merrillville/Hobart

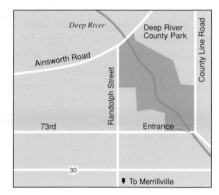

7 IMAGINATION GLEN PARK

Description: Five miles of hiking and cross-country ski trails provide wildlife viewing opportunities in wetland and forest habitats.

Viewing information: From August through October, there is a moderate probability of seeing migrating salmon and trout from a viewing/fishing platform in the southeast corner of the park. High probability of viewing deer throughout the year. Although rarely seen, coyotes, red foxes, and gray foxes all occur in the area. Rare plants and orchids may be seen along trails in certain seasons. Parking fee is required on weekends and holidays during the summer.

Ownership: Portage Park Department (219) 762-1675
Size: 223 acres **Closest town:** Portage

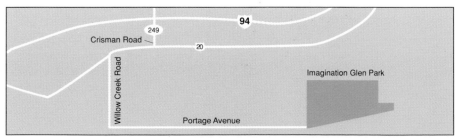

8 INDIANA DUNES STATE PARK

Description: Nationally famous sand dunes ecosystem created by the winds and waves along Lake Michigan. The continually shifting sands have created a great diversity of habitats, including huge sand ridges, upland forest, lowland marshes, and swamp forests. This area contains the most diverse group of plants and animals found in the Midwest. For more information about dunes, see the next page.

Viewing information: More than 300 bird species have been seen at the Dunes. Viewing is good in all seasons, but especially spring and fall. Moderate to high probability of viewing herons, night herons, egrets, and bitterns in the marshes. Thousands of gulls inhabit the beach areas in the summer. High probability of viewing frogs, turtles, snakes, and lizards during the summer. Entry fee required.

Directions: Pick up a property map at the entrance. Wildlife viewing is excellent throughout the park. Trail nine gives an excellent look at the different stages of dune development and the associated wildlife.

Ownership: Indiana DNR (219) 926-1952
Size: 2,182 acres
Closest town: Chesterton

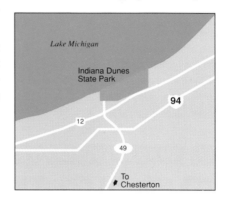

Ring-billed gulls are common along the Indiana Dunes. They use their long, narrow wings to glide on the updrafts created by wind coming off of Lake Michigan.
SCOTT NIELSEN

DUNES: THE BEACH IS JUST THE BEGINNING

Along the southern shore of Lake Michigan is a strip of nationally famous sand dune ecosystem called Indiana Dunes. Here you will find wide beaches, towering sand dunes, dead tree graveyards, wetlands, and numerous unique plants and animals thriving in this unusual habitat.

It all begins on the beach. For thousands of years the waves of Lake Michigan have pushed sand onto the shore, creating a beach. Gulls, raccoons, and red foxes scavenge the remains of fish and other animals that wash up on the shore. From the beach, sand is carried inland by the wind to the first line of plants. These plants catch it and cause it to pile up, creating the *foredune*.

Foredune plants such as marram grass have extensive networks of underground stems which hold the dunes in place. Cottonwood trees also grow on the foredune. As the stems of foredune plants and trees are buried by the growing dune, they begin to function as roots, and new stems continually push above the sand.

Different kinds of plants flourish on the back side of the dune, which is partially protected from the wind and waves. Little bluestem grass, sand cherry, and numerous wildflowers thrive here. Butterflies, bank swallows, and white-tailed deer are a few of the wildlife that live in this habitat. If the dune remains stable long enough, small *dune forests* of oak and hickory trees will become established, harboring red squirrels and box turtles.

The dune ecosystem is constantly altered by wind, water, and the unique plants that live here. "Graveyards" of blackened trees that have been buried with sand and then uncovered again are testimony to these constant changes.

Many people visit the Indiana Dunes just for the beaches—to sunbathe and observe the human "wildlife" that congregate here. But to a wildlife watcher or nature enthusiast, the beach is only the beginning.

9 INDIANA DUNES NATIONAL LAKESHORE

Description: The sand dunes, wetlands, bogs, and forests of the Indiana Dunes area make it one of the unique places in the entire country for wildlife watching and nature study. It was here that biologists first learned about biotic succession, or how one plant/animal community is replaced over time by another. For more information about succession, see page 36.

Viewing information: High probability of viewing all featured wildlife during certain seasons. The National Lakeshore has numerous holdings scattered along the Lake Michigan shoreline. The visitor center has maps of these areas and information about the interesting plant and wildlife communities found here.

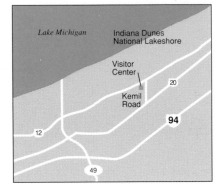

Ownership: National Park Service
(219) 926-7561
Size: 13,945 acres
Closest town: Chesterton/Michigan City

10 MOUNT BALDY

Description: Mount Baldy is part of the Indiana Dunes sand dune ecosystem. It is a large, wooded, sand mountain created by the strong winds that blow in from Lake Michigan. For more information about dunes, see the previous page.

Viewing information: Moderate to high probability of viewing hawks, sandhill cranes, warblers, and other birds as they migrate around Lake Michigan in the spring. Viewing is best in the middle of the day during March-April, on days when southerly winds prevail.

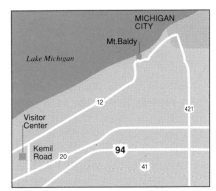

Ownership: National Park Service
(219) 926-7561
Size: 90 acres
Closest town: Michigan City

Description: More than 1,000 acres of wetlands located next to bottomland forest, agricultural fields, and upland hardwood forest.

Viewing information: One of the premier sites in the country for viewing sandhill cranes as they migrate during the fall and spring. In October and November, view up to 20,000 of these large wading birds on their way to Georgia and Florida. In March, more than 8,000 may be present, making their way back to northern breeding grounds. An observation platform offers a magnificent view of this annual spectacle. Bring binoculars or a spotting scope for best results. During the spring and summer, see ducks, geese, egrets, muskrats, and other wetland species on the marsh observation trail. *PUBLIC HUNTING AREA; PLEASE CHECK WITH MANAGER FOR AFFECTED AREAS AND SEASONS.* For more information on animal migrations, see the next page.

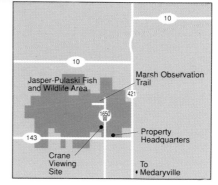

Directions: *Check in at the property headquarters and get a site map. Parking areas for the crane observation tower and marsh observation trail are both located on County Road 1650 W.*

Ownership: Indiana DNR (219) 843-4841
Size: 8,022 acres
Closest town: Medaryville

Thousands of sandhill cranes gather at Jasper-Pulaski Fish and Wildlife Area during their annual migrations. Providing areas such as this for resting and feeding during migration is critical to the survival of these magnificent birds. MARK ROMESSER

27

D. ROBERT FRANZ

MIGRATION: THE GRASS IS ALWAYS GREENER

Migration is the seasonal movement of wildlife from one location to another. Many different kinds of wildlife migrate—from monarch butterflies, to songbirds, to trout and salmon, to elk and caribou. But when people think of migration, most think of waterfowl—ducks, geese, and swans. Most folks in Indiana have seen Canada geese flying in V formations across the frosty November sky or the warming winds of March. But where are they going, and why?

Simply stated, animals migrate because the habitat in which they were born or hatched cannot sustain them through the entire year. Most waterfowl breed in northern lakes and wetland areas. These wet areas freeze in the winter, so food becomes unavailable. Similarly, there is not enough space or food available in the warmer, southern areas to sustain these populations year-round, so they are forced to continually pass back and forth between the two regions in order to survive.

Many migratory wildlife are able to return to precise locations year after year. Even more amazing, waterfowl often accomplish this task in spite of migrating at night and in heavy cloud cover. How do they know which way to go?

In daylight and clear skies, waterfowl find their way by using landscape features such as rivers and mountains. At night or in dense fog, some waterfowl are capable of using the position of the sun and stars to navigate. Still, some waterfowl migrate *between* cloud layers, unable to see the ground below or the stars above. Biologists think these birds may use the earth's magnetic field for navigation, but for now it remains one of nature's mysteries.

Migratory wildlife represent a dilemma to conservationists because they require conservation in two entirely different regions—often on different continents. For this reason, efforts to promote understanding of wildlife and cooperation between governments must be continued to ensure that these fascinating "globetrotters" remain part of our shared heritage.

Description: One of the last remnants of the Grand Kankakee Marsh, which once covered hundreds of thousands of acres. Located at the confluence of the Yellow and Kankakee rivers, the area includes extensive marshes, hardwood forests, and agricultural fields that are intentionally flooded in the spring and fall for wildlife. For more information about wetlands, see page 72.

Viewing information: The ten-mile trail provides opportunities for viewing wetland-related wildlife from your vehicle or on foot. High probability of seeing waterfowl during all seasons. Moderate probability of viewing shorebirds and wading birds anytime except winter. Sandhill cranes and bald eagles are seen occasionally. Beaver lodges are usually visible from the trail. Watch for beavers gathering food in the evening during fall. The trail may be closed due to flooding at any time—call ahead for trail status. Pick up a viewing trail map at the entrance. *PUBLIC HUNTING AREA. TRAIL IS CLOSED DURING THE FALL WATERFOWL HUNTING SEASONS—USUALLY LATE OCTOBER THROUGH EARLY DECEMBER.*

Ownership: Indiana DNR (219) 896-3522
Size: 3,328 acres   **Closest town:** Knox/North Judson

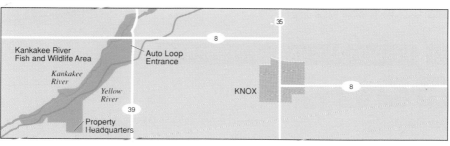

A "wet meadow" of aquatic plants provides homes for numerous kinds of wildlife at the Kankakee River Fish and Wildlife Area. Wetlands contain more different kinds of animals than any other type of habitat in the United States.

MARK ROMESSER

29

13 | LUHR COUNTY PARK

Description: Wetland area with six small islands surrounded by hardwood forest. Nine trails traverse the park, one of which leads to a wooden boardwalk and observation platform in the wetland. A paved, handicapped-accessible trail is also available.

Viewing information: High probability of viewing songbirds throughout the year. Moderate to high probability of seeing wood ducks, grebes, Canada geese, and other waterfowl, especially during spring and fall. In the spring, watch for geese nesting on the small islands, where they have some protection from land predators. Several species of frogs and turtles are seen frequently in the wetland. Deer are common along the woodland edges of the wetland. Visit the nature center for a trail map and further information.

Ownership: LaPorte County Parks & Recreation Dept. (219) 324-5855 or 326-6808, ex. 223

Size: 73 acres   **Closest town:** LaPorte

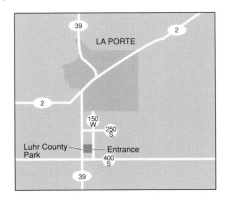

14 | ROUND LAKE NATURE PRESERVE

Description: Scenic, shallow, natural muck lake with undeveloped shoreline. Unique fen wetland area on the north side of the lake. For more information about wetlands, see page 72.

Viewing information: High probability of viewing great blue herons, rails, and waterfowl during all seasons except winter. Wetland-associated songbirds such as the hooded warbler are summer residents. During migration periods, there is a high probability of viewing marsh hawks and ospreys. Discover some unique plants and wildflowers in the fen wetland area north of the lake. No facilities.

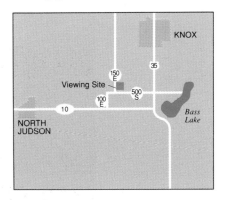

Ownership: Indiana DNR (317) 232-4052
Size: 140 acres
Closest town: North Judson

Description: Originally, this area was part of the Grand Kankakee Marsh, before being drained for agricultural use and later developed into an Army ammunition depot. Presently, it is owned and managed by the state Fish and Wildlife Division, which has restored much of the wetland resource. The Kankakee River, along with several lakes, wetlands, and drainage ditches, provides excellent aquatic habitat throughout the property. For more information about wetlands, see page 72.

Viewing information: High probability of viewing deer year-round. Drive slowly along the property roads at dawn or dusk for best results. High probability of seeing herons, egrets, and many waterfowl species during spring, summer, and fall. Muskrats are very common in the wetlands and drainage ditches. Watch for mink, raccoons, and beaver along the levees and ditches. *PUBLIC HUNTING AREA; PLEASE CHECK WITH MANAGER FOR AFFECTED AREAS AND SEASONS. THIS AREA WAS FORMERLY AN ARMY AMMUNITION DEPOT. THERE ARE SEVERAL WELL-MARKED, CONTAMINATED AREAS ON THE PROPERTY. OBEY ALL PROPERTY SIGNS.*

Directions: *Drive the property roads to view deer. Drive south on River Road to view the large wetland and the Kankakee River.*

Ownership: Indiana DNR (219) 393-3612
Size: 5,000 acres **Closest town:** LaPorte

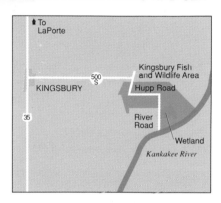

To
LaPorte

Kingsbury Fish
and Wildlife Area

500
S

KINGSBURY

Hupp Road

35

River
Road

Wetland

Kankakee River

Many people are unaware that the mink is a common resident of Indiana's wetland habitats. Mink are ferocious fighters, often preying on muskrats twice their size. Rabbits, snakes, birds, and even small snapping turtles are also prey for mink.

JAN L. WASSINK

16 TIPPECANOE RIVER STATE PARK

Description: A variety of habitats exist within this park which borders the Tippecanoe River. Hiking trails meander through oak forests, dry sand prairie, pine plantations, old fields, and marshes. The prairie remnants make good habitat for the endangered Franklin's ground squirrel. For more information about endangered species, see page 84.

Viewing information: High probability of viewing deer along the park roads and trails year-round. Many small mammal species may be seen here, including squirrels, beaver, red foxes, and thirteen-lined ground squirrels. Watch for the endangered Franklin's ground squirrel in sandy, tall-grass areas, especially in the evening. Waterfowl and other wetland-related wildlife are seen commonly in the waterfowl area and along the river. Pick up a park map at the entrance. Hiking trails are excellent for wildlife viewing. Entry fee required.

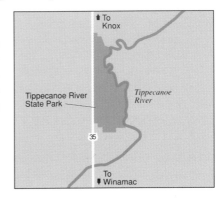

Ownership: Indiana DNR (219) 946-3213
Size: 2,761 acres
Closest town: Winamac

The wood duck is considered by many to be the most beautiful native North American duck. "Woodies" require tree cavities for nesting, so it is critical that landowners leave a few old "snag" trees standing near wetland habitats. SCOTT NIELSEN

Description: Spicer Lake was formed at the end of the last ice age when a huge block of buried ice melted here. Over time, biotic succession has changed the lake's appearance. About five acres of open water remain—the perimeter of the lake has become marsh and floating swamp forest. For more information about succession, see page 36.

Viewing information: High probability of viewing a variety of bird species, including warblers, flycatchers, nuthatches, and woodpeckers. Tremendous diversity of wetland plant species—from floating aquatic plants, to shrubs and bushes, to lowland trees. Snakes, frogs, and turtles are common. Look for large numbers of young snakes sunning themselves in the branches of lakeside shrubs in the spring. There is a handicapped-accessible boardwalk which extends out into the marsh, and several other hiking trails are available.

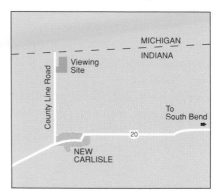

Ownership: St. Joseph County Parks Department (219) 654-3155
Size: 240 acres
Closest town: New Carlisle

Yellow warblers provide a bright splash of color that is a well-known sign of spring throughout Indiana. They prefer to nest in shrubby trees along streams and wetland areas.

JOHN SHAW

18 POTATO CREEK STATE PARK

Description: The diverse habitat types found in this park include a 327-acre lake, streambeds, wet fields, cattail marshes, old fields, and hardwood forest.

Viewing information: High probability of viewing deer along the park roads all year long. Viewing is especially good along the back side of the dam. Moderate to high probability of seeing great blue herons and kingfishers around the lake. Woodchucks, raccoons, squirrels, skunks, and opossum are common throughout the park. Excellent songbird and small mammal viewing at the nature center observation window year-round. Entry fee required.

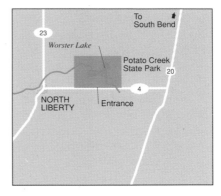

Ownership: Indiana DNR (219) 656-8186
Size: 3,840 acres
Closest town: Lakeville/North Liberty

Potato Creek State Park's Nature Center viewing window provides a wonderful opportunity to see many songbirds and small mammals. Hiking trails lead from the nature center to even more wildlife viewing opportunities along scenic Worster Lake.

POTATO CREEK
STATE PARK

Nature center viewing windows and feeding stations are great places to see wildlife up close and to learn about their habits and habitats; but don't forget to get out and look for these critters in their natural feeding stations—the great outdoors.

Description: One hundred sixty acres of rolling hills and mature hardwood forest within the South Bend city limits. Several small kettle holes created during the last ice age provide water for the wildlife found here. Shrubs, brush, and small trees behind the nature center provide excellent songbird habitat.

Viewing information: High probability of viewing several species of woodpeckers, including the large pileated woodpecker. These birds are attracted to large, old trees by the abundance of insects that live beneath the bark. The wildlife viewing window and the trail behind the nature center are good locations for viewing migrating warblers in April and May. Excellent number and diversity of woodland wildflower species found here from March through early June. High probability of viewing squirrels throughout the park all year. Other mammals seen less frequently include raccoons, opossum, foxes, and deer.

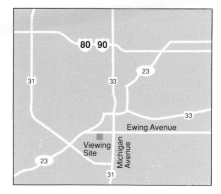

Directions: *View wildlife from park roads or walk the trails. Trailheads are located near parking areas throughout the park.*

Ownership: City of South Bend
(219) 284-9455
Size: 160 acres
Closest town: South Bend

The colorful pileated woodpecker is the largest woodpecker in Indiana—about the size of a crow. These striking birds require large, old trees in which they can excavate nest cavities and find food.
SCOTT NIELSEN

SUCCESSION: NOTHING STAYS THE SAME

Succession, in an ecological sense, refers to the predictable changes that occur in the plants and animals that live in any given area over time. Consider the fate of this abandoned farm field in southern Indiana:

1. Originally this field was a forest filled with tall beech and maple trees. When the forest was cleared for farming, it caused major changes in the plants and animals that could live here.

2. Later, when the field was abandoned, grasses, wildflowers, and other herbaceous plants took over the bare soil, which in turn attracted mice, sparrows, and other open-field animals.

3. Eventually shrubs and small trees became established in the field and shaded out the grasses and herbaceous plants. Rabbits and cardinals were among the animals that thrived in this new habitat.

4. Over the next twenty years, oak and hickory trees spread a dense canopy of leaves above the shrubs and brush, shading them out like the grasses before. Squirrels and forest birds gradually replaced the rabbits and shrub birds in the changing habitat. The first generation of oaks and hickories grew tall and mighty, but their seedlings had difficulty growing in the shade. Beech and maple seedlings, however, grew well in the shade. One by one, the old oaks and hickories fell and were replaced by beech and maple trees.

5. More than a century after the farm field was abandoned, it returned to beech and maple forest. Scientists call this the *climax* community—the group of plants and animals that will remain stable until disturbed by an outside force, such as wind, fire, flood, or human activity. Different regions of the world produce different types of climax communities, including prairie, desert, and rain forest.

In nature, nothing stays the same. The face of the land is continually being changed by natural or manmade events. Understanding the succession of plants and animals that follows these events is vital to understanding how wildlife will respond to changes in their environment.

Badgers live in prairie habitat and shrubby grassland areas. Their long claws and powerful shoulder muscles allow them to dig holes faster than a person with a shovel.

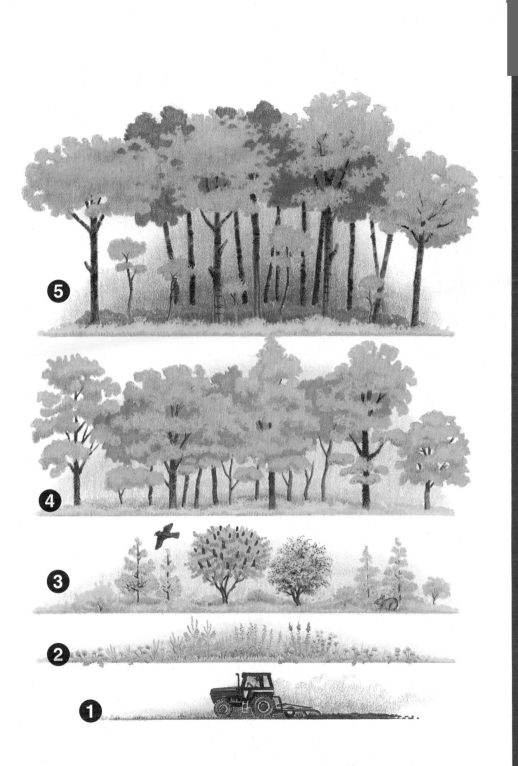

20 | MISHAWAKA FISH LADDER

Description: The last in a series of five fish ladders that allow trout and salmon from Lake Michigan to bypass manmade dams on the St. Joseph River as they migrate upstream. For more information about animal migrations, see page 28.

Viewing information: Moderate to high probability of seeing fish leaping at the foot of the dam in March and again from August through November. Viewing is best in the morning and evening, because fish try to avoid the direct mid-day sun by hiding in deeper areas of the river. Coho and chinook salmon migrate in September and October. Peak steelhead migration is in March and again in August and September. Fish also can be seen at a similar ladder located just a few miles away at the East Race in downtown South Bend.

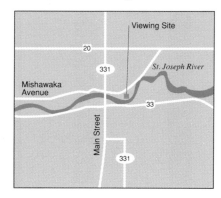

Directions: From the entrance to Central Park in Mishawaka, bear left on the main road to the parking lot at the very rear of the park. Walk through the stone fence and proceed up the path about 200 feet to the ladder.

Ownership: Indiana DNR (219) 829-6241
Size: One-half acre
Closest town: Mishawaka

The Mishawaka fish ladder and this ladder in South Bend allow steelhead and salmon to swim up these "stair-step" boxes to bypass the dams on the St. Joseph River.

ANDREW JOHNSTON/
INDIANA DNR

21 POTAWATOMI WILDLIFE PARK

Description: Ponds, wetlands, old fields, and bottomland hardwood forset are found at this site along the Tippecanoe River.

Viewing information: High probability of viewing shorebirds, herons, and several species of ducks and geese. Many songbirds are found here, including bluebirds, tree swallows, indigo buntings, and northern orioles. Beavers and deer are seen commonly in the park, especially in the evening. Look for beaver lodges in the wetlands. They look like piles of sticks floating in the water. The entrance to a lodge is underwater, to prevent land predators like foxes from getting inside. The park is open from dawn to dusk, except when the caretaker must be away. Call ahead if you wish to confirm your visit.

Ownership: Potawatomi, Inc.
(219) 498-6550
Size: 203 acres
Closest town: Tippecanoe/Bourbon

22 NAPPANEE ENVIRONMENTAL EDUCATION AREA

Description: Small wetland located alongside a beech-maple woodlot and grassland area.

Viewing information: High probability of viewing waterfowl during spring, summer, and fall. Red-tailed hawks nest in the woods and are often seen perching on the nature center roof. This location is a good vantage point from which they can hunt small mammals in the grassland area. Great-horned owls are common in the woods. High probability of viewing small mammals year-round, including muskrats, opossum, raccoons, and squirrels. Look for the unique black squirrels that are common in this area. Nature center to be completed in 1992. Call ahead for hours of operation.

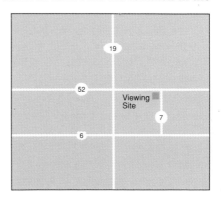

Ownership: Nappanee Parks & Recreation (219) 773-2112
Size: 35 acres   **Closest town:** Nappanee

23 BONNEYVILLE MILL COUNTY PARK

Description: Hiking trails wind through shrubby old fields, bottomland hardwoods, and river floodplain habitat surrounding an old grist mill on the Little Elkhart River.

Viewing information: The bottomland and river floodplain areas near the old mill are excellent for viewing mink, muskrat, raccoons, and opossum. High probability of viewing many different songbird species in the old field areas north of the river. Stop at the mill to pick up a site map and skier's guide. The skier's guide shows a piece of park property not included on the site map.

Ownership: Elkhart County Parks & Recreation Dept. (219) 534-3541
Size: 223 acres **Closest town:** Bristol

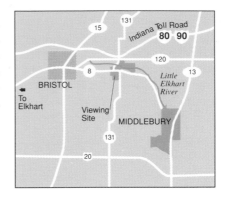

24 RIVER PRESERVE COUNTY PARK

Description: Scenic natural area along the Elkhart River. River corridor contains lowland hardwoods, wetlands, and river floodplain. For more information about riparian corridors, see page 67.

Viewing information: High probability of viewing deer, muskrats, and raccoons from spring through fall. Good waterfowl and shorebird viewing in spring and fall. Look for turtles and nonvenomous watersnakes sunning themselves on logs in the summer. Floating the river in a canoe from Benton to Baintertown is an excellent way to observe wildlife. Interpretive signs at the Benton Spillway and Baintertown access points show the locations of park property and other access points.

Ownership: Elkhart County Parks & Recreation Dept. (219) 534-3541
Size: 1,000 acres
Closest town: Benton/Goshen

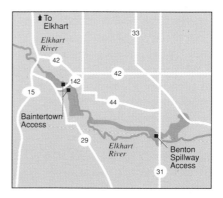

Description: This area contains a great diversity of habitats and land features, including flat to rolling fields, steep slopes of oak-hickory forest, shallow wetlands, and deep glacial lakes. For more information about habitat, see page 44.

Viewing information: Tri-County provides excellent viewing for all wetland-related wildlife species, especially waterfowl, shorebirds, aquatic mammals, and reptiles/amphibians. Wildlife can be viewed from the many roads that run throughout the property or by walking trails and access roads. Visitors should pick up a map at the property headquarters. *PUBLIC HUNTING AREA; CHECK WITH MANAGER FOR AFFECTED AREAS AND SEASONS.*

Directions: *Travel on State Road 13 to County Road 900 N. Turn east at the property sign and travel to the T junction at Hoss Hills Road. Turn right and proceed half a mile to the property headquarters.*

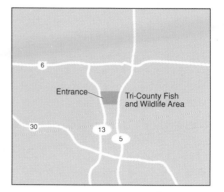

Ownership: Indiana DNR (219) 834-4461
Size: 3,400 acres
Closest town: North Webster

The painted turtle is the most widespread turtle in North America. They may be seen by the dozens sunning themselves on rocks and logs in lakes, ponds, and wetland areas.
SCOTT NIELSEN

26 | MERRY LEA ENVIRONMENTAL CENTER

Description: Numerous habitats occur here, including lakes, wetlands, old fields, prairie, and forest. All of these habitats may be viewed from the hiking trails that occur throughout the property. For more information about habitats, see page 44.

Viewing information: High probability of viewing a wide variety of songbirds year-round. Common small mammals include raccoons, skunks, chipmunks, and rabbits. Tiger swallowtail butterflies are common in July, and monarch butterflies may be viewed in the fall as they migrate south for the winter. A number of frogs, salamanders, snakes, and turtles may be seen here from spring through fall, including the rare Blanding's turtle. Visit the learning center and pick up a site map and checklists for the animals, birds, and plants of the area. Property gate open from dawn to dusk. Learning center open Mon.-Fri. 8 a.m. -5 p.m.

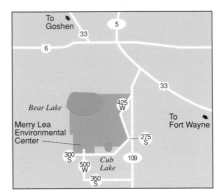

Ownership: Goshen College (219) 799-5869
Size: 1,150 acres
Closest town: Wolf Lake

27 | PIGEON RIVER FISH AND WILDLIFE AREA

Description: Long, narrow property along the floodplain and surrounding lowlands of Pigeon Creek and Pigeon River. Good aquatic habitat around the three dams and abandoned hydroelectric power raceways on the property.

Viewing information: Excellent waterfowl viewing during spring migration. High probability of seeing great blue herons, green herons, and kingfishers along the river. Large numbers of Canada geese nest on islands in the waterfowl resting area. Moderate probability of viewing ospreys in the wetland areas along the river. Deer are very common throughout the property. *PUBLIC HUNTING AREA; PLEASE CHECK WITH MANAGER FOR AFFECTED AREAS AND SEASONS.*

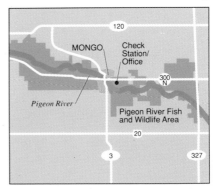

Ownership: Indiana DNR (219) 367-2164
Size: 11,500 acres
Closest town: Mongo

Description: Hiking trails wind through upland hardwood forest and around a seasonal wetland that holds water from spring through early summer.

Viewing information: Small mammals are abundant here. Look for raccoons, opossum, red squirrels, and fox squirrels. Moderate to high probability of viewing red-backed salamanders, wood frogs, and other amphibians in the seasonal wetland. The wetland area also has some unique plant communities, including the putty root orchid and several species of ferns. Visit the nature center for a trail map and to view squirrels and songbirds through an observation window.

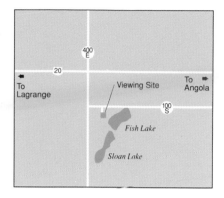

Ownership: LaGrange County Dept. of Parks & Recreation (219) 463-7825 or 463-4022

Size: 68 acres   **Closest town:** LaGrange

This wetland on the Pigeon River Fish and Wildlife Area has numerous small islands where Canada geese can nest in safety from foxes and other land predators. PHIL T. SENG

HABITAT: A PLACE CALLED HOME

Habitat is simply the place where an animal lives—its physical surroundings. Some people like to think of it as an animal's address in the environment. A habitat contains all the things an animal needs to survive and reproduce. These include food, water, and shelter, as well as hundreds of more subtle factors like temperature, moisture, and soil type.

Access to proper habitat is a necessity for wildlife. Each animal is adapted to living under a certain set of conditions, and if these conditions are not met, the animal will not be there for long. A squirrel must have woodland where it can find nuts to eat and trees in which to nest. A beaver requires shallow water where it can build a dam and lodge, and find bark and twigs to eat. You will not find a squirrel dog-paddling through a wetland, nor will you see a beaver chewing on a tree in the deep woods. The habitat just isn't right.

Many of Indiana's endangered species are endangered, not because their kind were killed, but because their habitats were altered or destroyed by human activity. Protecting habitat is a critical conservation goal. It ensures that a variety and abundance of wildlife will be around for future generations to enjoy.

29 CHAIN O' LAKES STATE PARK

Description: Beautiful series of connected kettle lakes nestled among steep, wooded hillsides. During the last ice age, glaciers pushed up huge mounds of earth in this area. As the glaciers receded, large, partially-buried blocks of ice were left behind. These blocks eventually melted to form lakes, and small rivers of water from the melting ice created the channels that now connect the lakes.

Viewing information: High probability of viewing great blue herons, green herons, and several waterfowl species during certain seasons. Many species of woodland and upland songbirds are present year-round. High probability of viewing deer from park roads and trails year-round. Red foxes and mink are seen occasionally along park roads at dusk, and several badger dens occur on the property. Entry fee required during the summer season. Follow park signs to the office or nature center to get a map of the roads and trails.

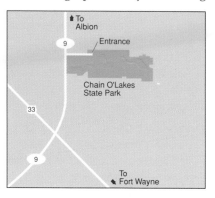

Ownership: Indiana DNR (219) 636-2654
Size: 2,678 acres **Closest town:** Albion

Get a new perspective on wildlife watching with a peaceful canoe trip through scenic Chain O'Lakes State Park.

RICHARD FIELDS/
INDIANA DNR

30 | BIXLER LAKE PARK WETLAND NATURE AREA

Description: Wetland and bottomland forest areas adjacent to Bixler Lake. Two wooden observation platforms along the edge of the wetland provide excellent wildlife viewing opportunities. A shrubby, old-field area provides food and cover for small mammals and songbirds.

Viewing information: Squirrels and raccoons are common in the wooded areas, and rabbits can be seen throughout the park. Low to moderate probability of viewing red foxes and mink from the wetland observation platforms at dawn and dusk. Wood ducks, mallards, and teal are common in the wetland. Look for Canada geese nesting on the numerous small islands during spring. Nesting on islands provides some protection from land predators. More than twenty-five species of wildflowers can be seen here from March through May. Pick up a site map at the trailhead. Entry fee required.

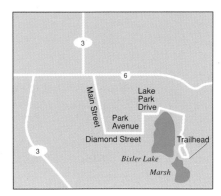

Ownership: Kendallville Park & Recreation Dept. (219) 347-1064

Size: 82 acres   **Closest town:** Kendallville

31 | FOX ISLAND COUNTY PARK

Description: This site contains wetland areas, dune forest, pine plantations, old fields, and bottomland hardwood forest. Trails meander throughout the park, and an observation platform is available at the wetland.

Viewing information: Over 200 species of songbirds have been recorded here; many are seen regularly at the nature center feeding station. Moderate probability of viewing red foxes, especially in the evening. High probability of viewing squirrels, woodchucks, chipmunks, rabbits, and other small mammals. Entry fee required during the summer. Pick up an area map at the nature center.

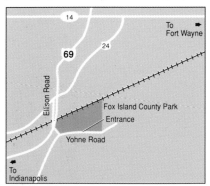

Ownership: Allen County Park & Recreation Board (219) 747-7846

Size: 605 acres

Closest town: Fort Wayne

REGION 2 - CROSSROADS

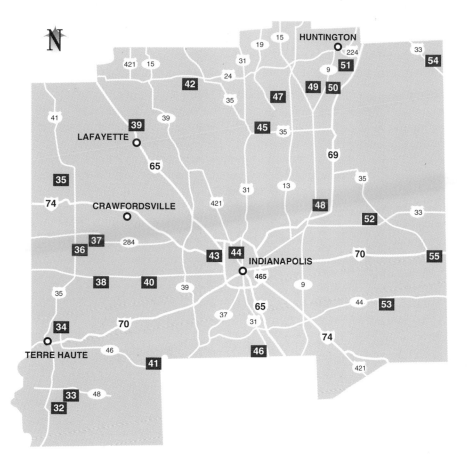

SITE 32 MINNEHAHA FISH AND WILDLIFE AREA	**SITE 44** WHITE RIVER PARKS
SITE 33 SHAKAMAK STATE PARK	**SITE 45** KOKOMO RESERVOIR
SITE 34 DOBBS PARK	**SITE 46** OLD CAMP ATTERBURY
SITE 35 PORTLAND ARCH NATURE PRESERVE	**SITE 47** MISSISSINEWA LAKE
SITE 36 TURKEY RUN STATE PARK	**SITE 48** KILLBUCK WETLAND
SITE 37 SHADES STATE PARK	**SITE 49** SWITCHGRASS MARSHES
SITE 38 RACCOON STATE RECREATION AREA	**SITE 50** MAJENICA MARSH
SITE 39 WABASH HERITAGE TRAIL	**SITE 51** HUNTINGTON LAKE KEKIONGA TRAIL
SITE 40 OSCAR AND RUTH HALL WOODS NATURE PRESERVE	**SITE 52** SUMMIT LAKE STATE PARK
SITE 41 MCCORMICK'S CREEK STATE PARK	**SITE 53** MARY GRAY BIRD SANCTUARY
SITE 42 CASS COUNTY FRANCE PARK	**SITE 54** KEKIONGA PARK
SITE 43 EAGLE CREEK PARK	**SITE 55** HAYES REGIONAL ARBORETUM

32 MINNEHAHA FISH AND WILDLIFE AREA

Description: Large area with a diverse mixture of habitat types and wildlife. Extensive grassland areas and brushy old fields are attractive to birds of prey. Riparian corridor of bottomland hardwoods along Busseron Creek bisects the property north to south. For more information on riparian corridors, see page 67.

Viewing information: High probability of seeing large congregations of waterfowl on the lakes and wetland areas in March and April. Herons and kingfishers are common in the wet areas. A rookery of nesting great blue herons can be seen from parking area H5 in spring. *DO NOT DISTURB NESTING HERONS—STAY ON THE ROAD.* On the north end of the property, grasslands are prime hunting grounds for hawks, owls, and harriers. Large numbers of short-eared owls may be viewed during fall and winter, and some nest here in early spring. Stop at the office for a map, and drive any of the county roads that traverse the property. The eight-mile-long Minnehaha Hiking Trail begins at the office, runs through all of the major habitat types on the property, and ends near Goose Pit Lake near County Road 450 N. *TRAIL IS NOT A LOOP.* Brochures for the trail should be available at the office in 1992. *PUBLIC HUNTING AREA; PLEASE CHECK WITH MANAGER FOR AFFECTED AREAS AND SEASONS.*

Ownership: AMAX Coal Company/ Indiana DNR (812) 268-5640
Size: 11,500 acres
Closest town: Sullivan/Dugger

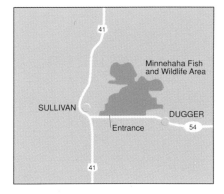

The striking coloration of the eastern meadowlark is a common sight in the prairie and grassland areas of Indiana. They nest on the ground, building loose domes of grass over shallow depressions in the soil.

JOHN SHAW

33 SHAKAMAK STATE PARK

Description: Three lakes nestled amid hardwood forest. The lakes have many fingers and inlets, and wildlife viewing from small boats can be excellent. Boat ramps and boat rentals are available.

Viewing information: Barred owls may be heard and occasionally seen near the fish cleaning station on Lake Shakamak. Northern goshawks have been sighted on Trail 3 near the service road. Limited probability of viewing red foxes throughout the park—one of the better spots is along Trail 2 at dawn or dusk. Drive slowly along the park roads for excellent deer viewing year-round. Dawn and dusk are best. Small mammals such as raccoons, chipmunks, and squirrels are very common in the park. Look for the albino squirrels along Trail 3, near the boat ramp. Albino animals have no pigment or color in their fur, making them appear completely white. Albino animals usually have difficulty surviving in the wild because their white fur is easily seen by predators. Entry fee required.

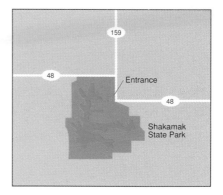

Ownership: Indiana DNR (812) 665-2158
Size: 1,766 acres
Closest town: Jasonville

Red foxes are active mostly at night, but you may see them at dawn or dusk. Technically, foxes are carnivores (meat eaters) but much of their diet consists of berries, fruits, nuts, and grasses.

JAN L. WASSINK

34 DOBBS PARK

Description: This park contains ponds, wetlands, pine forest, old-growth hardwood forest, and open field areas. Short, handicapped-accessible trail available near the nature center.

Viewing information: Excellent opportunity to view warblers and other migratory songbirds as they pass through the area in April and May. View songbirds, woodpeckers, and small mammals from the nature center observation window. Great blue herons, green herons, and kingfishers are common in the wet areas during summer. Flowering plants attract hummingbirds in July and August, and more than a dozen butterfly species—including tiger swallowtails, red admirals, painted ladies, and monarchs—may be seen from June through September, especially during August.

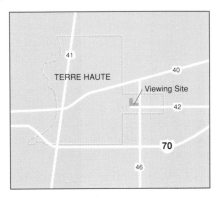

Ownership: Terre Haute Park & Recreation Department (812) 877-1095
Size: 105 acres
Closest town: Terre Haute

35 PORTLAND ARCH NATURE PRESERVE

Description: This site is named for a massive natural bridge carved into a sandstone rock formation by a tributary of Bear Creek. Rare and unusual plants grow amid the deep ravines and steep rock walls found here.

Viewing information: Frogs, turtles, and salamanders can be viewed along the rocky banks of Bear Creek. The slopes of the deep ravines are covered with mosses and lichens. Lichens (pronounced "likens") are actually a combination of algae and fungi that live together in one plant. Look for scattered beds of blueberry, huckleberry, and wintergreen. *MANY OF THE PLANTS FOUND HERE ARE RARE. DO NOT DISTURB THE VEGETATION.*

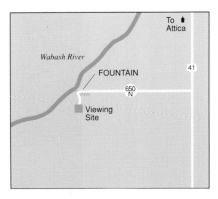

Ownership: Indiana DNR (317) 232-4052
Size: 292 acres   **Closest town:** Fountain

Description: Steep, rocky bluffs and scenic sandstone gorges along Sugar Creek. Ten hiking trails wind throughout the beautiful geological features of the park.

Viewing information: Good songbird viewing year-round. Look for woodpeckers, nuthatches, and other birds attracted to the large, old trees in the stands of virgin timber in the area. Large groups of turkey vultures ride the thermals or updrafts of air that rise up out of the valleys and gorges along Sugar Creek. Red-tailed hawks also are very common during summer. View longnose gar and other fish from the suspension bridge on Trail 1. Developed area of the park may be crowded from June through October. Visit the extensive nature center for more information on the wildlife found in the park and the surrounding area. Entry fee required.

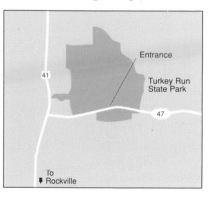

Ownership: Indiana DNR (317) 597-2635
Size: 2,382 acres
Closest town: Marshall

Watch for woodland wildlife in the deep green valleys and scenic gorges of Turkey Run State Park. Take a hike on any of the Park's trails for some wonderful wildlife viewing and nature study opportunities. MARK ROMESSER

37 SHADES STATE PARK

Description: Prominent overlooks and deep sandstone canyons along scenic Sugar Creek. One of the park's ten hiking trails leads to the Pine Hills Nature Preserve which borders the property. Both areas have impressive geological formations and stands of old-growth forest.

Viewing information: High probability of viewing turkey vultures and hawks on sunny days from spring through fall. As sunlight hits the rocky cliffs, it causes warm air currents, or thermals, to rise up out of the canyons. Birds spend many hours riding effortlessly on these thermals. Excellent viewing from Prospect Point and Lover's Leap. Squirrels, rabbits, raccoons, opossum, and other small mammals are common throughout the park. Moderate probability of seeing deer along park roads at dawn and dusk. Entry fee required.

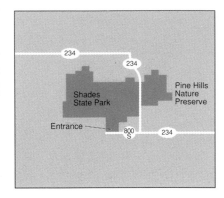

Ownership: Indiana DNR (317) 435-2810
Size: 3,082 acres
Closest town: Waveland

38 RACCOON STATE RECREATION AREA

Description: Trails and campgrounds in the mature hardwood forest along Cecil M. Harden flood-control reservoir.

Viewing information: Raccoons are very common here, along with woodchucks, squirrels, and other small mammals. Good songbird viewing along Trail 1. Feeding stations along area roads attract numerous songbirds during winter. Wild turkeys are often seen along the entrance road near the north shelter. Entry fee required.

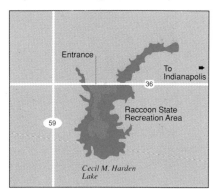

Ownership: Indiana DNR (317) 344-1412
Size: 4,065 acres
Closest town: Rockville

39 WABASH HERITAGE TRAIL

Description: Seven-mile linear trail along Burnett's Creek and the Wabash River from Tippecanoe Battlefield Park to the McAllister Park Golf Course. The trail crosses Burnett's Creek five times and crosses the Wabash River at the old Davis Ferry Bridge.

Viewing information: Squirrels, chipmunks, woodchucks, and songbirds are common in the wooded habitat along Burnett's Creek and in the Wabash River floodplain. Moderate to high probability of viewing great blue herons in spring, summer, and fall. Parts of the trail may be flooded, especially in spring and fall. Visit the nature center at the Tippecanoe Battlefield Park access point for more information about the wildlife and history of this area.

Directions: *Public access points for the trail are located at Tippecanoe Battlefield Park, Davis Ferry Park, and the McAllister Park Golf Course.*

Ownership: Tippecanoe County Parks Dept. (317) 463-2306 and Lafayette Parks Dept. (317) 447-9351

Size: 7.5-mile trail

Closest town: Lafayette/Battleground

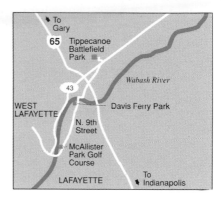

40 OSCAR AND RUTH HALL WOODS NATURE PRESERVE

Description: Large, old, white oak trees dominate the ridgetops in this mature forest, while sycamore, tulip poplar, and buckeye are most common in the many ravines and valleys.

Viewing information: Several species of woodpeckers are found in this area, including downy, hairy, red-headed, and pileated. They eat insects that live under the bark of old trees. High probability of viewing migrating warblers in the spring along Big Walnut Creek. Chipmunks and squirrels are common throughout the area.

Ownership: Indiana DNR (317) 232-4052

Size: 94 acres   **Closest town:** Bainbridge

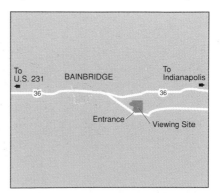

41 McCORMICK'S CREEK STATE PARK

Description: Indiana's first state park is a mixture of steep limestone canyons, waterfalls, heavily wooded ridgetops, hardwood forest, and shrubby field areas. Ridgetop hiking trails provide a close look at the birds and other wildlife that live in the very tops of the large, old trees growing along the steep slopes and valleys below.

Viewing information: More than 150 bird species have been sighted within the park boundaries. The spring songbird migration peaks in mid-May. For more information about animal migrations, see page 28. In the shrubby, second growth of the old rally camping area, many bird species can be viewed from April through September, and an abundance of butterflies, including the spicebush swallowtail and great spangled fritillary, can be seen in July and September. Deer are common along park roads and trails. High probability of seeing painted turtles and nonvenomous banded watersnakes sunning themselves along McCormick's Creek. Two-lined salamanders are also common under rocks along the creek. Entry fee required.

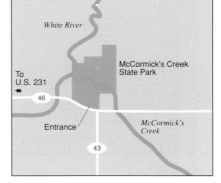

Directions: To view birds or butterflies in the old rally camping area, park at the campground office and proceed on foot through the campground to the service road next to Campsite 194. This road leads to the old rally camping area. Mowed trails provide excellent wildlife viewing.

Ownership: Indiana DNR (812) 829-2235 or 829-4344
Size: 1,833 acres   **Closest town:** Spencer

The black swallowtail butterfly is a beautiful reason to take afternoon walks through grasslands in summer. Butterflies and moths also play an important role in the pollination of many plants.

JULIA M. BECKER

42 CASS COUNTY FRANCE PARK

Description: Formerly an active stone quarry operation, this park now has an abundance of diverse habitat types, including a dry quarry, a crystal-clear quarry lake, wetlands, lowland forest, upland forest, old fields, and the Wabash River.

Viewing information: Unique opportunity to view large paddlefish, up to six feet in length, in the clear quarry lake. See bluebirds, titmice, chickadees, wrens, finches, and many other songbirds in the fields and wooded areas. High probability of viewing deer along park roads and trails year-round. The pond on the west end of the park is home to literally thousands of turtles. Several species of nonvenomous snakes are common here. Watch for the eastern hognose snake in particular. When approached, this reptile will hiss and puff up its head and neck in an effort to bluff the intruder. If touched, it will promptly roll over on its back and play dead. Entry fee required.

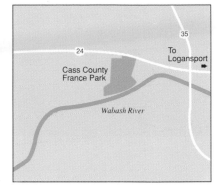

Ownership: Cass County Park & Recreation Board (219) 753-2928
Size: 400 acres
Closest town: Logansport

The raccoon is an omnivore—it will eat nearly anything. The nimble fingers of these masked bandits can easily remove young birds and squirrels from tree cavities, as well as hot dogs and potato salad from coolers.

KEN TAYLOR

Although they look more like skunks or badgers, the closest relatives to the raccoons are the bears. Raccoons and bears both walk flat on the soles of their feet—just like people.

55

FOX SQUIRREL
BY JOHN SHAW,
HARDWOOD FOREST
BY RICHARD FIELDS/
INDIANA DNR

CARRYING CAPACITY: HOW MANY IS TOO MANY?

Biologists use the term *carrying capacity* to describe the number of animals a given piece of land or water can sustain over time. Consider a forest of oak and hickory trees—fox squirrels live in this forest, and each female is capable of producing between three and ten young squirrels per year. You'd think that before long, the place would be overrun with squirrels—but it's not. The key is that there are only so many nut trees, den cavities, and other resources to go around in this forest, so there are only so many squirrels that can "make a living" here. The number of squirrels able to survive is the forest's *carrying capacity* for squirrels. When the number of squirrels born is greater than the carrying capacity of the forest, the surplus animals will either fall prey to predators, die of starvation or disease, or try to move to other areas that are not yet at capacity.

Like most things in the natural world, carrying capacity is not constant. A bumper crop of hickory nuts may temporarily increase the carrying capacity of the forest, while a drought or fire may temporarily decrease it.

The carrying capacity of the land or a body of water is different for each kind of animal that lives there. Obviously there are more ants in the forest than squirrels, just as there are more squirrels than deer.

Knowledge of carrying capacity is critical to the conservation of wildlife populations. For instance, a herd of wild bison requires thousands of acres of open prairie to survive, while a population of fox squirrels will thrive in a forty-acre woodlot. Biologists use carrying capacity to determine how much habitat is required to support the minimum number of animals necessary to maintain a healthy population.

43 EAGLE CREEK PARK

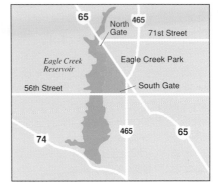

Description: More than eight miles of hiking trails surround a 1,300-acre lake located only a few minutes from downtown Indianapolis. Steep, wooded bluffs overlook a waterfowl sanctuary on the north end of the lake.

Viewing information: Moderate to high probability of viewing pintails, shovelers, scaup, wood ducks, and other waterfowl in the spring and fall. High probability of viewing Canada geese all year. The shallow north end of the lake offers excellent waterfowl viewing. In dry years, large mud flats are exposed on the north end, which attract shorebirds and wading birds. Bring binoculars or a spotting scope to the North Overlook for the best view. Bald eagles are seen occasionally along the lake in January. Red-tailed hawks, rough-legged hawks, and northern harriers can be seen throughout the summer. Visit the nature center for a map and more information. Entry fee required. Park is open from dawn to dusk.

Ownership: Indianapolis Dept. of Parks & Recreation (317) 293-4827
Size: 5,250 acres
Closest town: Indianapolis

The white crescent on the face of this duck identifies it as a male blue-winged teal. The female is a mottled brown color which helps keep her concealed while nesting. Both have a powder-blue wing patch. SCOTT NIELSEN

44 WHITE RIVER PARKS

Description: Holliday and Marrott Parks offer some wonderful natural areas on the White River a few minutes from downtown Indianapolis. Oak and hickory trees spread across the broad ridges and steep slopes leading down to the river. Hiking trails meander throughout the wooded areas.

Viewing information: High probability of viewing songbirds year-round, including wrens, flycatchers, warblers, vireos, thrushes, and woodpeckers. Prothonotary warblers and yellow-crowned night herons have been seen at Holliday Park. Wood ducks, mallards, Canada geese, and herons are common along the river. Wildflower viewing is excellent in April and May. Look for marsh marigold, Virginia bluebell, hepatica, and purple-flowering raspberry.

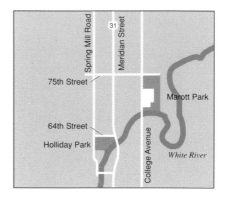

Ownership: Indianapolis Dept. of Parks & Recreation (317) 924-7072
Size: Holliday Park: 88 acres;
Marrott Park: 83 acres
Closest town: Indianapolis

45 KOKOMO RESERVOIR

Description: Open fields, brushy old fields, and hardwood forest surrounding a small reservoir near downtown Kokomo. A hiking trail runs through bottomland hardwoods between the dam and the small park area located on the south side of the lake. A handicapped-accessible observation/fishing pier is available.

Viewing information: Moderate to high probability of viewing numerous species of ducks and geese in the coves and inlets of the lake. Herons and egrets are occasionally seen in areas with heavy shoreline vegetation. Squirrels and chipmunks are common along the trail, and rabbits are abundant in the grassy field areas.

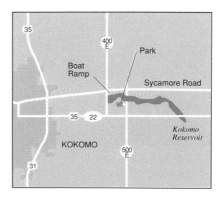

Ownership: Indiana American Water Co./ Kokomo Parks & Recreation Dept. (317) 452-0063
Size: 800 acres   **Closest town:** Kokomo

Description: Formerly a U.S. Army infantry training camp, the area is now made up of Atterbury Fish & Wildlife Area and Johnson County Park. Both areas remain criss-crossed with abandoned blacktop roads that provide excellent songbird viewing from the car. Grasses, shrubs, bushes, and small trees have taken over the area, creating ideal habitat for songbirds and small mammal species.

Viewing information: Excellent songbird viewing year-round. Flycatchers, swallows, wrens, vireos, warblers, sparrows, and woodpeckers are but a few of the many types of birds seen. Slowly drive the abandoned roads with binoculars for best results. High probability of seeing numerous waterfowl species in the many lakes and wetlands on the area. Small mammals such as rabbits, woodchucks, and ground squirrels thrive in this brushy habitat, attracting predators such as coyotes, red foxes, and birds of prey. Johnson County Park has a songbird viewing blind and hiking trails through different habitats. Honker Haven on the Atterbury Fish and Wildlife Area has an observation platform and camera blind for waterfowl viewing/photography. *ATTERBURY FISH AND WILDLIFE AREA IS A PUBLIC HUNTING AREA. PLEASE CHECK WITH MANAGER FOR AFFECTED AREAS AND SEASONS. JOHNSON COUNTY PARK IS A SAFETY ZONE YEAR-ROUND.*

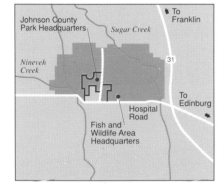

Ownership: Indiana DNR (812) 526-2051 / Johnson County Parks Dept. (812) 526-6809
Size: 6,000 acres
Closest town: Edinburgh

The badger is active mostly at night, and prefers to sleep during the day. Once found only in the prairies of northwest Indiana, badgers now can be seen occasionally in central and southern Indiana as well.

RICHARD FIELDS/
INDIANA DNR

47 MISSISSINEWA LAKE

Description: Large flood-control reservoir surrounded by agricultural fields, steep limestone cliffs, and dense hardwood forest. There is a short overlook trail on the northeast end of the property which provides a panoramic view of the lake and some of its wildlife. Trees which lined the old river channel still stick out above the water here, providing prime perching locations for aquatic birds.

Viewing information: From late September through early November, there is a high probability of viewing black cormorants perched on the old, dead trees in the lake. High probability of seeing various waterfowl species in this area spring and fall. Bring binoculars or a spotting scope for best viewing. *PUBLIC HUNTING AREA; PLEASE CHECK WITH MANAGER FOR AFFECTED AREAS AND SEASONS. RECEIVES HEAVY USE IN THE FALL.*

Directions: *To reach the cormorant viewing site, travel south on State Road 13. Turn left on County Road 925 S., then right on County Road 100 W. Proceed to a T in the road where you will turn left on County Road 1000 S. Proceed about .75 mile to the gravel road and parking area on the right.*

Ownership: Indiana DNR (317) 473-6528
Size: 14,000 acres   **Closest town:** Peru

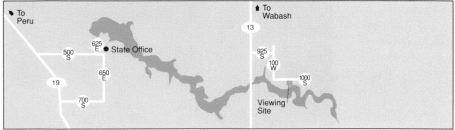

Turkey vultures have a disgustingly effective way of protecting their nests from predators–they regurgitate foul stomach contents on any intruder! Vultures play an important role in the ecosystem by eating dead and decaying animals.

48 KILLBUCK WETLAND

Description: Wetland area and three-mile, handicapped-accessible river greenway trail near downtown Anderson.

Viewing information: Mallards and Canada geese are common in this area spring, summer, and fall. Moderate probability of seeing wood ducks in the spring and fall. Beaver, muskrats, and mink are common in the wetland area. These animals are mostly nocturnal, but occasionally can be seen at dawn and dusk. Entire length of the existing greenway trail is handicapped-accessible. An additional seven-mile trail connecting Killbuck Wetland with Mounds State Park on the east side of Anderson is scheduled for completion by 1993.

Ownership: Anderson Parks & Recreation Dept. (317) 646-5753
Size: 3-mile loop trail
Closest town: Anderson

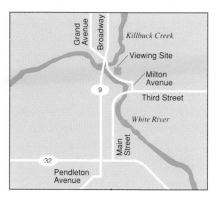

The large, beautiful great blue heron silently stalks fish and frogs in shallow water. This elegant bird is dependent on Indiana's few remaining wetlands for survival.
SCOTT NIELSEN

49 SWITCHGRASS MARSHES

Description: Wetland complex located behind the Lost Bridge West State Recreation Area on Salamonie flood-control reservoir.

Viewing information: Excellent location for viewing wetland-related birds. More than forty species of shorebirds and wading birds have been seen here, including sandpipers, yellowlegs, herons, and egrets. About a dozen species of ducks may be seen in the spring. Muskrats are common in the marsh—they construct burrows in the earthen dams, or build houses in the body of the wetland. The entrances to these houses are underwater, keeping land predators out. Entry fee to the State Recreation Area required.

Directions: *From State Road 105, turn west onto County Road 400 S. Enter the Lost Bridge West State Recreation Area and follow the signs to the Apple Orchard Campgrounds. The marshes are on the south side of the campgrounds.*

Ownership: Indiana DNR (219) 468-2125
Size: 11 acres   **Closest town:** Huntington

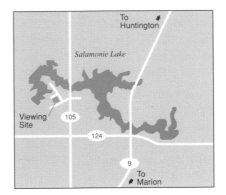

50 MAJENICA MARSH

Description: Wetland complex bordered by open fields, hardwood forest, and an arm of the Salamonie flood-control reservoir. Hollow trees standing in the marsh have nesting cavities that may be used by wood ducks and hooded mergansers.

Viewing information: More than forty species of shorebirds and wading birds have been seen here. High probability of viewing herons and egrets in summer and fall. Numerous waterfowl species use this area, and hooded mergansers may nest here in spring. Look for deer along the wooded edge of this marsh at dawn and dusk. Moderate probability of seeing ospreys, also known as fish hawks.

Ownership: Indiana DNR (219) 468-2125
Size: 7 acres   **Closest town:** Huntington

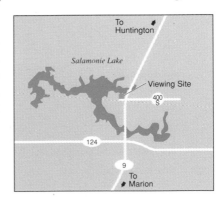

51 HUNTINGTON LAKE KEKIONGA TRAIL

Description: Ten-mile loop hiking trail wraps around the main body of Huntington flood-control reservoir. Trail passes through hardwood forest, agricultural fields, shrubby old fields, and shoreline habitat.

Viewing information: Small mammals are common along the trail. Look for squirrels, chipmunks, raccoons, and rabbits. Although not often seen, striped skunks occur throughout the property. Moderate probability of viewing deer along the trail at dawn and dusk. Coyotes and red foxes are seen occasionally along field borders and grassy areas. Trailhead is located at the observation pavilion northeast of the dam. The portion of the trail on the north side of the lake is in a safety zone. *SOUTHERN LEG OF THE TRAIL RUNS THROUGH A PUBLIC HUNTING AREA. CHECK WITH PROPERTY MANAGER FOR AFFECTED SEASONS.*

Ownership: Indiana DNR (219) 468-2165
Size: 8,322 acres   **Closest town:** Markle

52 SUMMIT LAKE STATE PARK

Description: Large expanse of open grassland mixed with shrubby old fields, small woodlots, and a 600-acre lake. Three trails in the park offer excellent wildlife viewing on the lake and in the grasslands.

Viewing information: The expanse of open grassland habitat here is somewhat unique in the state park system. More than 100 songbird species have been sighted here. Waterfowl and wading birds use the lake frequently, especially the wetland area in the northeast corner of the property. Loons are occasionally seen here in winter. Entry fee required.

Ownership: Big Blue River Conservancy/ Indiana DNR (317) 766-5873
Size: 2,552 acres
Closest town: New Castle

AGRICULTURE: CHANGING THE LAND, CHANGING WILDLIFE

Ever since the first settlers cleared a few trees to plant corn, the need to produce food has had a major impact on land use in this country. With changes in land use have come sweeping changes in the kinds of wildlife that inhabit the land.

Some wildlife, such as the bison that once roamed the prairie of northwest Indiana, require large expanses of unbroken habitat. Land divided into a patchwork of agricultural fields and small wood lots is unsuitable for these animals. However, other wildlife such as white-tailed deer thrive in agricultural areas. They are able to make use of the farm fields that have become common among the forests, wetlands, and other native habitats.

Agriculture, like any other event that changes the landscape, has benefitted some kinds of wildlife at the expense of others. It is only when crop fields become large and unbroken that nearly all wildlife suffer. Without any trees, shrubs, or fence rows to provide cover and protection from predators, a huge farm field is uninhabitable by most animals and remains largely unused—a wildlife desert. Misuse of chemical pesticides and herbicides can also be disastrous to wildlife populations.

Agriculture has played a key role in Indiana's history—a role which continues today. Wildlife are strongly linked with agricultural practices here. Understanding this linkage is important for maintaining healthy wildlife populations.

53 MARY GRAY BIRD SANCTUARY

Description: A mixture of ponds, wetlands, creeks, fields, and hardwood forest. Service roads, hiking trails, and fire lanes provide good access into all the different habitat types on the property.

Viewing information: High probability of viewing songbirds throughout the year. Good opportunity to view warblers in May and again in October as they migrate to and from their spring breeding grounds. For more information about animal migrations, see page 28. Bats are very common in the summer. Watch them catch mosquitoes and flying insects against the sky at dusk. Moderate to high probability of viewing hawks, including red-tailed, broad-winged, Cooper's, and sharp-shinned. Frogs, turtles, and salamanders are common in the wet areas, and a number of nonvenomous snake species are found throughout the property, including rat snakes, racers, water snakes, and hognose snakes.

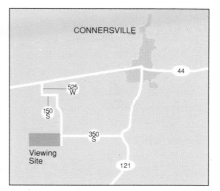

Ownership: Indiana Audubon Society (317) 827-0908
Size: 660 acres
Closest town: Connersville

The cardinal is a year-round resident in Indiana, and its presence brings color and cheerful song to the long, cold winter months.
JOHN SHAW

54 KEKIONGA PARK

Description: River greenway and forested park area along the Saint Mary's River corridor near downtown Decatur. For more information about riparian corridors, see page 67. The greenway begins at Kekionga Park, crosses the river on a scenic, abandoned railway trestle, and ends at the Decatur Parks and Recreation Office at Monroe Street. The entire greenway is handicapped-accessible.

Viewing information: High probability of viewing great blue herons during spring, summer, and fall. Moderate to high probability of seeing kingfishers, yellowlegs, sandpipers, and other associated bird species in certain seasons. Big brown bats and little brown bats are common throughout the park in June and July. Watch them catching mosquitoes in the evening twilight. Parts or occasionally all of this area may be flooded during periods of high rainfall.

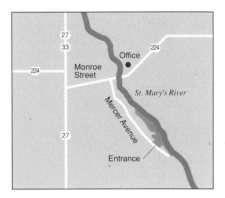

Ownership: Decatur Parks & Recreation Department (219) 724-2520
Size: 55-acre park; .75-mile river greenway
Closest town: Decatur

55 HAYES REGIONAL ARBORETUM

Description: This site is a living collection of the plants, shrubs, and trees native to the Whitewater River drainage basin in Indiana and Ohio. Some of the species found here are rare in Indiana. A 3.5-mile auto tour winds through mature forest, abandoned pasture, and an old gravel pit wetland area.

Viewing information: Rare to moderate probability of viewing red and gray foxes along the trails at dawn and dusk. Deer are common throughout the park. See a great diversity and abundance of the flowering plants, shrubs, and vines native to this area in spring and summer. Wildflower viewing is best in late April. Visit the nature center for information on the diverse plant life found here.

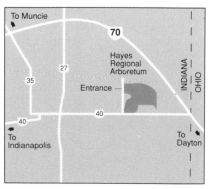

Ownership: S.W. Hayes Research Foundation, Inc. (317) 962-3745
Size: 355 acres   **Closest town:** Richmond

RIPARIAN CORRIDORS: ALONG THE FLOWING WATER

Riparian corridor is the technical name given to a creek, stream, or river and the riverbank or floodplain alongside it. These corridors are typically long and narrow and are associated with flowing water.

Because water is so important to all forms of life on earth, riparian corridors often contain a great variety and abundance of wildlife. These corridors also serve as wildlife travel lanes between other blocks of habitat that have become separated by farm fields, urban areas, or other human activity.

Rivers transport and deposit stones, sand, soil, and nutrients in predictable ways. The plant and animal communities found in riparian corridors develop in response to these patterns. When humans alter the natural state of the river by constructing dams, digging straight channels to replace meandering riverbeds, or removing large amounts of water for irrigation, the plant and animal communities are drastically affected, often in negative ways.

Many of the waterways in this country have been changed from rivers and streams into little more than "earthen canals"—perfectly straight, cleared of all riverbank vegetation, and muddied with prime topsoil on its way to the ocean. The plants and trees in natural riparian corridors lessen the impact of human activity and serve human needs by:

- Stabilizing the riverbanks and reducing soil erosion
- Absorbing run-off water, reducing the likelihood of flooding
- Trapping soil particles in run-off water, reducing siltation

Riparian corridors are ever-changing associations of water, soil, plants, and animals. Like wetlands, they are extremely valuable to wildlife, and like wetlands, they are being destroyed at an alarming rate by development. Protection and enhancement of riparian corridors is vital to wildlife and to people.

REGION 3 - HILL COUNTRY

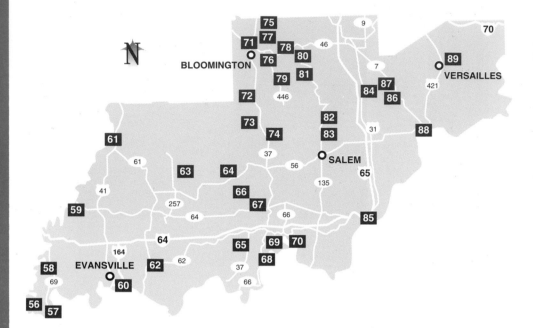

Description: One of the few cypress sloughs remaining in the Ohio and Wabash River valleys. This site actually consists of two separate swamp communities—bald cypress swamp and overcup oak swamp. Trails pass through floodplain hardwood forest before reaching a boardwalk which extends out into the bald cypress swamp.

Viewing information: High probability of viewing many different songbird species along the trails and on the boardwalk. Watch for the prothonotary warbler and blue-gray gnatcatcher. Shorebirds are very common throughout the swamp. Many have long, stilt legs and long, slender bills which allow them to wade in shallow water and probe the soft earth for worms, insects, and other small food items. No facilities.

Ownership: Indiana DNR (317) 232-4052
Size: 585 acres
Closest town: Mount Vernon

Hairy woodpeckers are found in forests from coast to coast. Woodpeckers use their short, stiff tailfeathers as natural "kickstands," to support their weight as they prospect for insects in the bark of old trees.
SCOTT NIELSEN

A woodpecker has a thick skull and special "shock absorber" around its brain which allow it to literally beat its head against trees all day long searching for insects that live beneath the bark.

57 HOVEY LAKE

Description: This area contains agricultural fields, marshes, and a 1,400-acre backwater lake along the Ohio River. *AREA IS SUBJECT TO FLOODING IN LATE WINTER AND EARLY SPRING.* The lake is full of old, flooded timber. The area contains typical southern-swamp plant and tree communities.

Viewing information: Fantastic wildlife viewing area. High probability of viewing waterfowl from January through March. Most common species are mallards, black ducks, wood ducks, and Canada geese. Numerous species of shorebirds may be seen in the marshes and wetland areas throughout the property. Hundreds of cormorants often congregate near the boat ramp in fall. Hundreds of thousands of crows roost here from November through March. Banded watersnakes and red-bellied watersnakes are common in the lake. Annual "turtle migration" occurs in May and June, and hundreds of turtles may be seen crossing the property roads and fields. *PUBLIC HUNTING AREA. PLEASE CHECK AT THE PROPERTY HEADQUARTERS FOR AFFECTED AREAS AND SEASONS.*

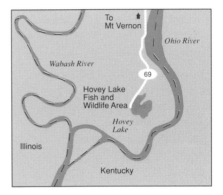

Ownership: Indiana DNR (812) 838-2927
Size: 4,400 acres
Closest town: Mount Vernon

A wooden box provides a nesting cavity for wood ducks at Hovey Lake Fish and Wildlife Area. Wood ducks require cavities for nesting, and will use these boxes readily.

RICHARD FIELDS/
INDIANA DNR

58 HARMONIE STATE PARK

Description: Rolling, wooded hills and open grasslands leading down to the Wabash River floodplain. Hiking trails and bicycle trails available.

Viewing information: Deer are common throughout the park. Slowly drive the park roads for excellent viewing and photographic opportunities. Moderate probability of seeing coyotes—watch for them along roads and field borders at dawn and dusk. Shorebirds and waterfowl may be viewed along the Wabash River. Spring and fall are the best seasons for waterfowl. A boat ramp is available, and wildlife watching along the undeveloped park shoreline and river island may be excellent. Entry fee required.

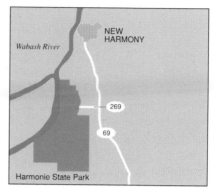

Ownership: Indiana DNR (812) 682-4821
Size: 3,465 acres
Closest town: New Harmony

59 GIBSON LAKE WILDLIFE HABITAT

Description: Two trails on this site provide wildlife viewing opportunities on the bayous of Coon Creek and on a shallow, wetland impoundment.

Viewing information: High probability of viewing mallards and Canada geese in the shallow wetland area throughout the year. Herons, egrets, and cormorants may be seen along Coon Creek or in the wetland. Bluebirds, tree swallows, finches, and rabbits are common in the grassy upland areas surrounding the wetland. Watch along wetland edges in the morning or evening for possible sightings of deer, raccoons, opossum, or mink. Photographic blind available on the wetland area. Visitors must sign an admission agreement to enter, and persons under eighteen must have an admission agreement signed by a parent or guardian.

Directions: *From the PSI Energy main entrance on State Road 64, drive one-half mile, cross a railroad track, and immediately turn right. Stop at the security station to sign-in.*

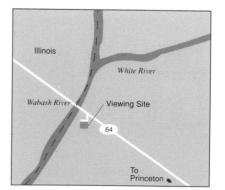

Ownership: PSI Energy (317) 838-1625
Size: 160 acres   **Closest town:** Princeton

WETLANDS: LIFE IN ABUNDANCE

We hear the word *wetlands* often these days. But what are wetlands, and why all the fuss? Simply stated, wetlands are just what you might expect: land that is wet, at least part of the time. All wetlands are associated with shallow water and aquatic plants. There are several different kinds of wetlands, and each has unique characteristics that make it different from the others. The types of wetlands found in Indiana include:

Marsh—The most common type of wetland. Contains fresh water, small plants, and shrubs.

Swamp—Basically the same as a marsh, except the dominant vegetation is trees instead of shrubs and small plants.

Bog—Receives little fresh water. Decaying plants cause the water to become acidic. May contain a floating mat of specialized plants growing in a ring around a small portion of open water.

Fen—The rarest of Indiana's wetlands. Associated with underground water supplies, such as seeps or springs. Contains specialized plants adapted for life in an alkaline water environment.

Wetlands are extremely valuable to wildlife, supporting a greater variety of animals than any other kind of habitat in the country. More than half of all endangered species in the U.S. rely on wetlands.

Wetlands are also important to people:

Flood control—Wetlands reduce flooding by storing storm water and releasing it gradually.

Water quality—Wetlands catch soil that erodes from the land, especially farmland. They also remove up to 90% of the phosphorous and nitrate compounds (soap and fertilizer) in run-off water, and are capable of detoxifying heavy metals, toxic chemicals, and disease agents.

Groundwater recharge—Wetlands can purify and recharge the wells and wellfields used by people for drinking supplies.

Prior to settlement, Indiana had almost 5.5 million acres of wetlands. Today, nearly 90% of those wetland acres have been lost as a result of human activities. Protecting the remaining wetlands and restoring some of those lost are critical wildlife conservation goals in Indiana and throughout the country.

Once thought to harbor evil spirits and death, wetlands are now known to be brimming with life, and extremely valuable to society.

60 WESSELMAN WOODS NATURE PRESERVE

Description: More than 200 acres of virgin bottomland hardwood forest located within the Evansville city limits. This is how much of the Ohio River Valley looked before the Midwest was settled. Trails, boardwalks, and nature center are handicapped-accessible.

Viewing information: Outstanding site for songbird viewing. More than 130 bird species have been identified in the area. During the first two weeks of May, thousands of birds pass through the preserve as they migrate to their northern breeding grounds. Excellent winter songbird viewing from the nature center observation window. Moderate probability of viewing deer on the trails, especially at dawn and dusk. Although rarely seen, red foxes, gray foxes, and coyotes visit the area occasionally. Squirrels, raccoons, opossum, and other small mammals are common throughout the preserve.

Directions: From the Wesselman Park entrance on Boeke Avenue, follow the main road as it bears to the right. There is a separate sign and parking lot for the nature preserve at the rear of the park.

Ownership: City of Evansville (812) 479-0771
Size: 200 acres   **Closest town:** Evansville

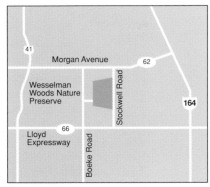

The deer mouse is an important strand in the food web. It produces numerous offspring, and so provides food for foxes, owls, snakes, and other animals.
JOHN SHAW

61 OUABACHE TRAILS PARK

Description: Steep, wooded hills and low, open fields along the Wabash River floodplain.

Viewing information: High probability of viewing raccoons year-round. Brown bats are common here. Watch them catch flying insects near the floodlights in the developed area of the park. Bald eagles and ospreys are occasionally seen perched in trees along the river. Indigo buntings, rose-breasted grosbeaks, and many other songbirds may be seen on the trails. Hike the woodland trails from March through May to find numerous varieties of spring wildflowers, including violets, lilies, phlox, and bloodroot. Park nature center is open Monday through Friday, from 8 a.m. until 5 p.m.

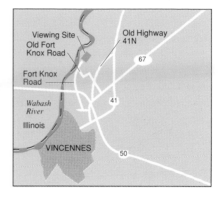

Ownership: Knox County Parks & Recreation Dept. (812) 882-4316
Size: 254 acres   **Closest town:** Vincennes

62 SCALES LAKE PARK

Description: This site contains hardwood forest, brushy old fields, and pine plantations surrounding a sixty-six-acre lake. Handicapped-accessible campsites, trails, and boat ramp are available.

Viewing information: Squirrels, chipmunks, and raccoons are seen commonly on the trails and at the campsites. Deer may be viewed on the trails, especially in the fall. A careful observer may see a red or gray fox in the woods or along field edges at dawn or dusk. Ducks and geese are often seen on the lake in spring and fall. Park is open 6 a.m. to 10 p.m. from Memorial Day through Labor Day. The remainder of the year the hours are variable. Call ahead to confirm. Entry fee required.

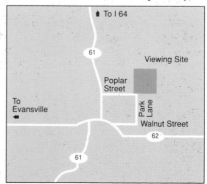

Ownership: Warrick County Parks & Recreation Department (812) 897-6200
Size: 400 acres   **Closest town:** Boonville

63 GLENDALE FISH AND WILDLIFE AREA

Description: This site contains forests, agricultural fields, wetlands, and shrubby, open areas surrounding a 1,400-acre lake. The east fork of the White River forms the area's southern boundary.

Viewing information: The large amount of shrubby, open area on this site attracts sparrows, thrushes, wrens, and other songbirds. American kestrels, also known as sparrow hawks, are often seen perched on telephone lines watching surrounding grasslands for insects and small mammals. High probability of seeing red-tailed hawks soaring above the open fields during summer. These birds are well-named; watch for a flash of red-orange color as the afternoon sun catches the tail feathers of a "red tail" turning lazy circles in the sky. High probability of viewing ducks, geese, herons, and other aquatic birds on Dogwood Lake and in the Himsel bottoms. *PUBLIC HUNTING AREA. CHECK WITH PROPERTY MANAGER FOR AFFECTED AREAS AND SEASONS.*

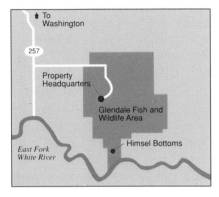

Ownership: Indiana DNR (812) 644-7711
Size: 8,000 acres
Closest town: Montgomery

Screech owls are small birds, less than ten inches in total length. They may be gray, brown, or reddish in color, with bright yellow eyes. They hunt at night for insects and small mammals.
JAN L. WASSINK

64 PAW PAW MARSH

Description: Flooded bottomland hardwood forest along an oxbow of Lost River. Surrounding lowlands contain hardwood forest, a white pine plantation, and shrubby, old field areas.

Viewing information: High probability of viewing beavers and muskrats during spring, summer, and fall. Beavers are mostly nocturnal, meaning they are active primarily at night. However, they often emerge from their lodges before sundown. Deer are common in this area—look for their narrow trails along the river. Herons and egrets may be seen on the marsh and along the river. Winter songbird viewing is excellent in the pine plantation and shrubby, old fields between the parking lot and the marsh. No facilities. *HUNTING PERMITTED ON PUBLIC LANDS IN AREA. CONTACT THE INDIANA DNR FOR AFFECTED SEASONS.*

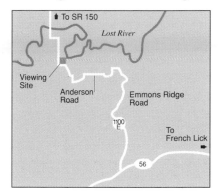

Ownership: U.S. Forest Service (812) 358-2675
Size: 5 acres   **Closest town:** Shoals

65 INDIAN/CELINA LAKES

Description: Two clear lakes nestled in the wooded hills of the Hoosier National Forest. Roads and trails run through native hardwood forest mixed with pine plantations, and provide excellent wildlife viewing opportunities.

Viewing information: Woodland songbirds are common in this area. Winter viewing is especially good in the pine plantations. High probability of seeing deer along the roads and trails, and beside the lakes in early morning. Hawks and turkey vultures are often seen soaring above the lakes. Bald eagles and ospreys are seen occasionally perched in shoreline trees during winter. Hike the trails in April and May to see an abundance of spring wildflowers.

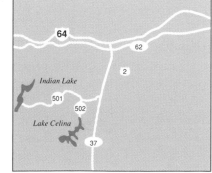

Ownership: U.S. Forest Service (812) 547-7051
Size: 12-mile loop trail
Closest town: Saint Croix

66 PATOKA LAKE OVERLOOK

Description: Scenic hillside overlook of the main body of Patoka Lake flood-control reservoir. *FALL COLORS ARE SPECTACULAR.*

Viewing information: High probability of viewing bald eagles perched in shoreline trees during winter. Eagles may catch fish in the shallow bays of the lake, but will also feed on dead fish and waterfowl along the shoreline. Ospreys, also called fish hawks, are seen here occasionally. An osprey is better at catching fish than an eagle, but the eagle is larger and will often rob the osprey of its catch. Moderate probability of seeing great blue herons flying over this viewing site, and waterfowl may be seen here during migrations.

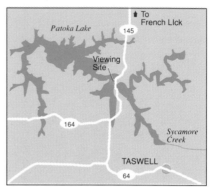

Ownership: Indiana DNR (812) 685-2464
Size: 1 acre **Closest town:** French Lick

67 SYCAMORE CREEK MARSH

Description: Long, shallow finger of the Patoka Lake flood-control reservoir. When the reservoir water level is low, this area becomes a large, shallow wetland and mud flat.

Viewing information: High probability of viewing mallards, gadwalls, widgeons, teal, grebes, and other waterfowl species during the spring migration. Herons, egrets, snipe, woodcock, and other wetland bird species may be seen here in certain seasons. Red-tailed hawks are common in the summer; rough-legged hawks may be seen during winter. Moderate probability of seeing muskrats in the wetland. Squirrels and chipmunks are seen frequently in the woodlots along the wetland. *PUBLIC HUNTING AREA; CHECK WITH PROPERTY MANAGER FOR AFFECTED AREAS AND SEASONS.*

Directions: From Taswell, turn north at the sign for the "Little Patoka Boat Ramp." After crossing Sycamore Creek bridge, turn left into the gravel parking area.

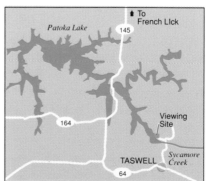

Ownership: Indiana DNR (812) 685-2464
Size: 20 acres
Closest town: French Lick

FOOD WEBS: WE'RE ALL CONNECTED

Every plant and animal on earth requires energy or food to survive, and this energy flows from one life form to another in complex cycles. Because of these cycles, all living things are related to each other.

The *food chain* illustrated above provides a simplified look at an energy cycle. The sun in the center provides the energy which supplies all life on earth. The green plants in cell 1 are called *producers:* they convert sunshine and soil nutrients into plant material. This stored energy is converted into animal material when the leaves and seeds are eaten by the small animals in cell 2. Cell 3 contains the *carnivores,* or meat eaters, that convert the energy stored in the small animals into their own body tissues. When the carnivores die, their bodies are decomposed into the soil, providing nutrients for more green plants in cell 1. Each cell represents a link in the chain, and the chain is a loop that continually repeats itself.

This simple chain becomes much more interesting and complicated when you consider that many animals such as foxes and raccoons eat fruits, berries, and other plant foods in addition to meat. Therefore, you could add another arrow to the diagram from cell 1 to cell 3. The micro-organisms that cause carnivores to decompose and return to the soil also do the same for plants and small animals. Before long, arrows are pointing from every cell into every other cell. The end result looks more like a web than a chain, which is why these relationships are often called *food webs*. Food webs illustrate the complex interrelationships that exist between living things and their environments. Whenever a single strand in the web is affected, the entire web is affected.

68 BUZZARD'S ROOST OVERLOOK

Description: High, prominent lookout above the Ohio River. This site offers a beautiful view of the river, and the patchwork of farmland across the river in Kentucky. *FALL COLORS ARE SPECTACULAR.*

Viewing information: High probability of viewing hawks and turkey vultures soaring on thermal air currents rising up from the river valley during summer. Bald eagles are often seen along the river in winter. Woodland songbirds are common in the forested areas along the river. *HUNTING PERMITTED ON PUBLIC LANDS IN THE AREA. CONTACT INDIANA DNR FOR AFFECTED SEASONS.*

Ownership: U.S. Forest Service (812) 547-7051
Size: 80 acres
Closest town: Magnet/Alton

69 LITTLE BLUE RIVER

Description: This scenic fourteen-mile stretch of the Little Blue River runs through wooded hills from the town of Sulphur to the Ohio River near Alton.

Viewing information: High probability of viewing wood ducks and herons along the river. Squirrels may scold you from the protective limbs of large sycamore trees as you float by in a canoe or rowboat. Listen for Carolina wrens and other songbirds of the river bottoms. This area is especially beautiful in springtime, when the riverbanks are colored in the blue, yellow, pink, and white hues of spring wildflowers.

Directions: Northern access point: one mile north of Sulphur. Southern access point: from Alton, travel north about two miles to a T in the road. Turn right and proceed about .75 mile.

Ownership: U.S. Forest Service (812) 547-7051
Size: Fourteen-mile river float
Closest town: Sulphur

Description: This site contains numerous trails and old fire roads in the rolling hills of the Harrison-Crawford State Forest. The Blue River flows through Wyandotte Woods before emptying into the Ohio River which forms the area's southern boundary.

Viewing information: Songbirds such as warblers, finches, sparrows, and woodpeckers are common throughout the property. See ruby-throated hummingbirds at the nature center observation window. High probability of seeing deer on trails and along the roads. Several kinds of snakes may be seen in the area, including the venomous copperhead. DO NOT DISTURB SNAKES. For many years, snakes have been the victims of bad publicity. They play an important role in the ecosystem, and rarely pose a threat to humans unless provoked. High probability of viewing hawks and turkey vultures at the Ohio River overlook. Bring binoculars or a spotting scope for best viewing. Bald eagles are seen along the river during winter. Entry fee required.

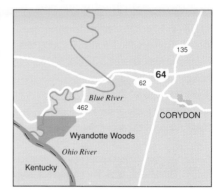

Ownership: Indiana DNR (812) 738-8232
Size: 2,100 acres
Closest town: Corydon

It's hard to believe, but the regal white-tailed deer was once eliminated from Indiana. A re-introduction program in the 1940s and years of careful management have now made the deer a common resident in every Indiana county.

MARK PICARD

71 GRIFFEY RESERVOIR

Description: Forested hills lead down to a wetland area along Griffey Reservoir. Numerous trails meander through the forest and wetland areas.

Viewing information: High probability of viewing a large congregation of migrating warblers in May. Beavers and muskrats may be seen in the lake and wetland. Beavers are mostly nocturnal, which means they are active primarily at night, but they may be seen in the morning and evening. Muskrats may be seen throughout the day. Painted turtles and nonvenomous northern watersnakes are very common in the lake and wetland. Watch for both sunning themselves on floating logs during the summer.

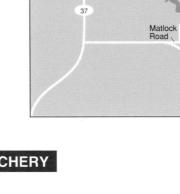

Ownership: City of Bloomington/ Bloomington Parks and Recreation Department (812) 332-5220
Size: 1,200 acres
Closest town: Bloomington

72 AVOCA STATE FISH HATCHERY

Description: Trails run along spring-fed rearing ponds, small creeks, and upland forest at this warmwater fish hatchery.

Viewing information: Rearing ponds contain small bass, bluegill, redear sunfish, and crappie. View large rainbow trout brood stock year-round in spring-fed ponds. Moderate probability of viewing kingfishers and great blue herons along the creeks and ponds. Ospreys have been seen catching trout out of the holding ponds. Follow the trails up steep ridges and across broad plateaus of upland forest. Woodland songbirds and small mammals are common on the trails, and deer are seen occasionally. Property is open seven days a week, from sunrise to sunset. Office is open from 8 a.m. to 5 p.m., Monday through Friday.

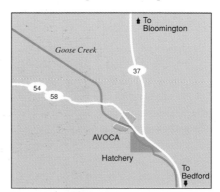

Ownership: Indiana DNR (812) 279-1215
Size: 43 acres
Closest town: Avoca/Bedford

Description: This site contains an underground river that flows through limestone caverns and passageways. View cave wildlife from a boat on the longest navigable underground river in the United States.

Viewing information: High probability of viewing blind cave crayfish throughout the viewing season. Moderate to high probability of seeing blind cave fish in late September and October. Because these animals live in total darkness, functional eyes and protective coloration serve no purpose. Therefore, the first animals born here without color or eyes were better able to survive because they could spend the energy needed to build and maintain eyesight on other things, such as feeding and reproduction. These advantages gave the blind and colorless animals higher survival and reproductive rates than their "normal" siblings. Therefore, over time, the entire population became blind and colorless. Bats may also be seen here, especially in October. From May 1 through September 30, caverns are open every day, 9 a.m. to 5 p.m., E.S.T. Caverns are open on weekends during April and October. Bring a light jacket. Entry fee required.

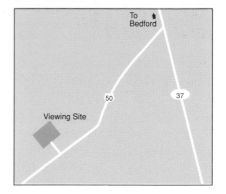

Ownership: Bluesprings Caverns, Inc.
(812) 279-9471
Size: 15 acres   **Closest town:** Bedford

See blind crayfish like this at Bluesprings Caverns and Spring Mill State Park. Because color serves no purpose in the totally dark cave world, these animals have no pigment in their bodies— they appear white.
BLUESPRING CAVERNS

ENDANGERED SPECIES: AND THEN THERE WERE NONE

An endangered species is a plant or animal whose population has declined to the point that it is in danger of becoming extinct—gone from the earth forever.

Extinction is nothing new. Plants and animals were becoming endangered and extinct long before people had any impact on their populations. However, people are responsible for the present *rate* at which species are becoming endangered and extinct. Scientists estimate that before recorded history, the earth probably lost one species every thousand years. Today, the earth loses more than one species every year—possibly as many as one species every day—and the rate continues to increase.

It is critical that endangered species be protected from extinction. The federally endangered peregrine falcon, for instance, has been absent from Indiana since 1878, and is now being re-introduced by the Indiana Department of Natural Resources. But it is even more important to prevent other species from becoming endangered in the first place. Both recovery and prevention can be achieved through the protection and management of habitat. For example, the Franklin's ground squirrel, which is endangered in Indiana, requires a prairie habitat to survive. Because so little prairie exists in Indiana, protecting those patches that remain will play a crucial role in preserving the Franklin's ground squirrel and other prairie wildlife.

In the long run, wildlife conservation is best served by shifting emphasis from the protection and management of single species to the conservation of entire ecosystems—whole groupings of plants and animals that are interrelated with each other, and with the land. This is commonly known as conservation of biological diversity, or *biodiversity*.

Endangered species are symptoms of a larger problem. Restoring endangered species on a case-by-case basis is treatment for the symptoms; conservation of biodiversity is the cure.

74 SPRING MILL STATE PARK

Description: This site contains a diversity of habitats and wildlife. There is a pristine tract of virgin hardwood forest, pine plantations, open field areas, spring-fed streams, a manmade lake, and a limestone cave system.

Viewing information: This is an excellent site for wildlife viewing and nature study. Follow trail number three through virgin hardwood forest—most of southern Indiana looked like this before settlement. Woodpeckers, creepers, nuthatches, and other songbirds are attracted to the large, old trees found here. Squirrels, chipmunks, and raccoons are common, especially near the campgrounds. Short-tailed shrews are also common, but are very secretive and rarely seen. They root around among the leaves and plants on the forest floor looking for insects, worms, and mice. Rainbow trout and brown trout can be viewed in the spring-fed stream at the Pioneer Village. Take a twenty-minute boat trip through Twin Caves to see blind cave fish, blind crayfish, cave crickets, and bats. Boat trips are offered 9 a.m. to 6 p.m. E.S.T. from mid-April through October. During summer, the park is crowded and these trips are booked by 10 a.m. each day, so come early. Visit the nature center for more information on the wildlife and history of this area. Entry fee required.

Ownership: Indiana DNR (812) 849-4129
Size: 1,319 acres   **Closest town:** Mitchell

Spring-fed streams running through the Pioneer Village at Spring Mill State Park contain brown trout and rainbow trout. Trout thrive in the cold water that flows out of springs and caves.

RICHARD FIELDS/
INDIANA DNR

75 THREE LAKES TRAIL

Description: Ten-mile loop trail that winds throughout the rolling, wooded hills of Morgan-Monroe State Forest. In pre-settlement days, most of southern Indiana was covered with hardwood forest like this. *FALL COLORS ARE SPECTACULAR.*

Viewing information: High probability of seeing deer, squirrels, and woodland songbirds along the trail year-round. Deer have a keen sense of smell and often will smell you long before they see you. Therefore, hike into the wind whenever possible. Near the Bryant Creek picnic area, the trail runs through a five-acre wildlife opening which is especially good for songbird viewing. Watch for ruffed grouse in this area as well. Trail is moderate to rugged and can be hiked in a single day. *PUBLIC HUNTING AREA. PLEASE CHECK AT MANAGER'S OFFICE FOR AFFECTED AREAS AND SEASONS.*

Directions: *Visit the property headquarters for a map of the Three Lakes Trail and other trails in the area.*

Ownership: Indiana DNR (317) 342-4026
Size: Ten-mile loop trail
Closest town: Martinsville

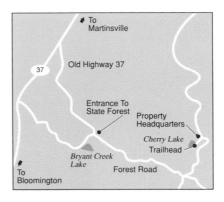

The eastern chipmunk may be seen in open woodlands, forest edges, and brushy areas throughout Indiana. Although it spends most of its time on the ground, it will not hesitate to climb tall oak trees when acorns are ripe.
SCOTT NIELSEN

Description: A series of shallow marshes along the north fork of Lake Monroe flood-control reservoir. Wooden observation platform is available along one of the marshes.

Viewing information: Many species of waterfowl, including mallards, scaup, widgeons, and teal, use this area to rest and feed as they migrate north in the spring and south in the fall. Waterfowl viewing may be best in spring when male ducks are in their colorful breeding plumage. *THIS AREA IS SUBJECT TO SPRING FLOODING.* Great blue herons are common in these wetlands. High probability of viewing songbirds year-round. In August and September, large patches of cardinal flower bloom along the wetland edges, attracting many hummingbirds. *PARTS OF MARSH COMPLEX ARE OPEN TO PUBLIC HUNTING. ACCESS TO CERTAIN AREAS IS RESTRICTED FROM OCTOBER 1 THROUGH APRIL 15.*

Directions: *From Bloomington, travel east on State Road 46 about three miles. Turn right onto Kent Road, proceed about .5 mile, then turn right again onto McGowan Road. Drive about two miles to the marsh complex.*

Ownership: Indiana DNR (812) 837-9546
Size: 500 acres
Closest town: Bloomington

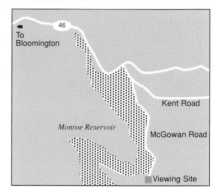

A meandering river channel has created numerous backwaters and wonderful wetland habitat near Lake Monroe. Wetlands such as this provide homes for more than half of the endangered species in the United States. RICHARD FIELDS/INDIANA DNR

77 RIDDLE POINT PARK

Description: The developed portion of Riddle Point Park is a beach and recreational area on Lake Lemon. However, visit the park office for directions and permission to enter the "Little Africa" viewing area nearby. This site contains grasslands, shrubby second-growth, and wetlands along the undeveloped portion of Lake Lemon's shoreline.

Viewing information: A host of sparrows, warblers, wrens, and other songbirds may be seen in the grassy, old field areas of "Little Africa" during certain seasons. Hawks and harriers are common here also. The wetland areas along the lake may be visited by herons, egrets, cormorants, bitterns, and a variety of ducks and geese. The water of Lake Lemon is fairly clear, and the spawning beds of largemouth bass and bluegill may be seen in shallow water during spring. These fish create shallow depressions in lake-bottom mud in which they lay their eggs. Watch for adult fish guarding these spawning beds from salamanders and other small fish that try to eat the eggs. Entry fee required.

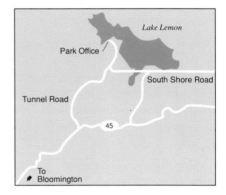

Ownership: City of Bloomington/ Bloomington Parks and Recreation Department (812) 332-5220
Size: 100 acres
Closest town: Bloomington

The leopard frog's green and black body is excellent camouflage for hiding in shoreline plants and mud. Frog eggs, tadpoles, and adults are all staple food items for many creatures in the wetland food web.

JOHN SHAW

Description: Roads and hiking trails traverse more than 20,000 acres of hardwoods and pine plantations in this state forest. A twenty-acre wetland at the upper end of Yellowwood Lake provides good wildlife viewing in beautiful surroundings.

Viewing information: Hike around Yellowwood Lake for some excellent wildlife viewing. Ducks and geese use the lake and wetland area for resting and feeding on their annual migrations. Spring is best for waterfowl viewing. Herons may be seen in the wetland from spring through fall. High probability of viewing woodland songbirds around the lake and throughout the property year-round. Deer are common on the lake shoreline in early morning. Limited probability of seeing foxes along forest roads in the morning or evening. *PUBLIC HUNTING AREA. PLEASE CHECK AT THE PROPERTY MANAGER'S OFFICE FOR AFFECTED AREAS AND SEASONS.*

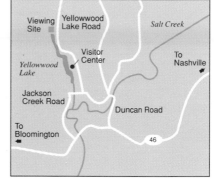

Ownership: Indiana DNR (812) 988-7945
Size: 22,500 acres
Closest town: Nashville

The opossum is related to the kangaroos of Australia. It is the only North American marsupial. Opossums are important garbage disposers, as much of their diet is made up of dead animals.

JOHN SHAW

Like the kangaroos of Australia, the female opossum has a pouch on her belly. Up to fourteen baby opossums occupy the pouch at a time. The young are so tiny at birth, the whole litter will fit into a tablespoon!

79 HICKORY RIDGE TRAILS

Description: Hiking trails and primitive roads follow the densely-wooded ridges and valleys of the Charles Deam Wilderness Area within the Hoosier National Forest. The trails pass by numerous streams and wildlife ponds and may be followed to the shores of Monroe Lake flood-control reservoir.

Viewing information: Squirrels, chipmunks, raccoons, and opossums are common along the trails. Raccoons prefer areas near the lake or along creeks and streams. Deer may also be seen along the trails. Walk quietly in the morning or evening for best results. Climb the Hickory Ridge Lookout Tower for a breathtaking view of the surrounding countryside. *FALL COLORS ARE SPECTACULAR.* The tower provides a good view of hawks and turkey vultures soaring above the treetops during summer. Hike down to the shore of Lake Monroe to see a variety of wading birds, turtles, and frogs. Cricket frogs are especially melodious on early summer evenings. *HUNTING PERMITTED ON PUBLIC LANDS IN THE AREA. CONTACT INDIANA DNR FOR AFFECTED SEASONS.*

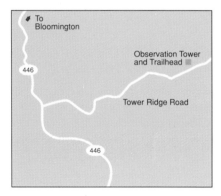

Directions: *Unmarked hiking trails are available throughout the area. Contact the U.S. Forest Service for a trail brochure.*

Ownership: U.S. Forest Service (812) 358-2675
Size: 60 miles of unmarked trails
Closest town: Bloomington

The American kestrel, or sparrow hawk, is a beautiful, small falcon that often perches on telephone wires or "hovers" along mowed highway corridors. Kestrels are common in Indiana, but most people just pass by without noticing them. SCOTT NIELSEN

Description: Rolling hills of mature hardwood forest. Numerous scenic vistas and overlooks. *FALL COLORS ARE SPECTACULAR.* White-tailed deer are very common here, as well as a variety of songbirds. *PARK IS CROWDED DURING OCTOBER.*

Viewing information: High probability of seeing deer along park roads in any season. Winter and spring viewing are recommended to avoid crowds. The nature center observation window is an excellent spot to view songbirds, squirrels, raccoons, and deer. Hike the park trails to see deer and other wildlife in a more natural setting. Entry fee required.

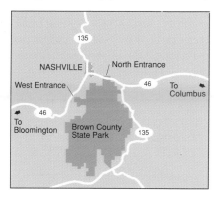

Ownership: Indiana DNR (812) 988-7185 or 988-6406
Size: 15,696 acres
Closest town: Nashville

Brown County State Park is one of the many sites in Indiana where fall colors are spectacular. Colors reach their peak in October, and are most vivid when the days are bright and sunny, but cool.

MARK ROMESSER

81 MAINES POND

Description: Small pond located near open grasslands, shrubby old fields, cedar thickets, and small woodlots. A buried natural gas pipeline runs behind the pond, and the mowed pipeline corridor attracts songbirds and small mammals.

Viewing information: High probability of viewing meadowlarks, bluebirds, sparrows, bobwhite quail, and many other open-ground bird species in certain seasons. Wild turkeys have become very common in this area. In May and June, watch for hen turkeys leading broods of young birds called poults into the grassy areas to feed on insects. Adult turkeys eat mostly seeds, fruits, and nuts, but poults need the high protein content of insects to sustain their rapid growth. Deer may be seen on the edges of the pipeline corridor at dawn and dusk. Prairie grasses and wildflowers are abundant in the open areas during spring and summer. *PUBLIC HUNTING AREA. CONTACT INDIANA DNR FOR AFFECTED SEASONS.*

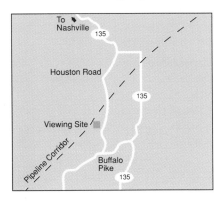

Ownership: U.S. Forest Service
(812) 358-2675
Size: 5 acres
Closest town: Freetown

A wild turkey gobbler "struts his stuff." Wild turkeys were once eliminated from Indiana, but through re-introductions and careful management, the Indiana Department of Natural Resources has restored this regal bird to much of the state.
BRENT PARRETT

Description: Four interconnected trails meander through the rolling, wooded hills that border Starve Hollow Lake. Trails range from easy to rugged. Information about each trail is listed at the main trailhead in the campground.

Viewing information: High probability of viewing squirrels, chipmunks, and numerous songbirds on all of the trails. Deer and raccoons may be seen along the trails or on the shoreline of Starve Hollow Lake. Wild turkeys and ruffed grouse are common in the forested areas. Ducks and geese may use the protected coves and inlets of the lake during their spring and fall migrations and throughout the summer months.

Directions: From the entrance to Starve Hollow State Recreation Area, follow the main road to the campground visitors parking lot. Walk east from the parking lot until you reach the lake, then turn left. Proceed through the campground until you reach the comfort station. Turn right and continue through the campground until you reach the trailhead near Campsite 46. Total distance from parking lot to trailhead is .4 mile.

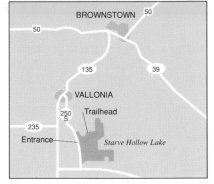

Ownership: Indiana DNR (812) 358-3464
Size: 4.1 miles of trails
Closest town: Vallonia

Woodchucks dig burrows in pasture land, and in earthen embankments along forests and crop fields. Many animals use woodchuck burrows for safety from predators and extreme weather.

BILL LEA

93

83 DELANEY CREEK PARK/KNOBSTONE HIKING TRAIL

Description: Delaney Creek Park is the northern trailhead for the fifty-eight-mile Knobstone Hiking Trail. The park contains rugged, wooded hillsides and an eighty-eight-acre lake with flooded timber at the east end. Knobstone Trail runs along the knobstone escarpment through the densely-wooded hills and valleys of southern Indiana. Five trailheads access the trail before it ends at Deam Lake Recreation Area just north of New Albany.

Viewing information: In Delaney Creek Park, view waterfowl and wading birds on the lake. Watch for ospreys, also called fish hawks, perched on the flooded timber at the east end of the lake. Along the Knobstone Trail, there is a high probability of viewing songbirds, squirrels, and other small woodland animals. Take a long hike on this trail to see the beauty and experience the solitude of the dense hardwood forest that once covered most of southern Indiana. Moderate probability of seeing deer, ruffed grouse, and wild turkeys on the trail and in the park. Entry fee required at the park. Call the Indiana DNR for a topographic map of Knobstone Trail.

Ownership: Delaney Creek Park: Washington County (812) 883-5101; Knobstone Trail: Indiana DNR (317) 232-4070
Size: 354-acre park; 58-mile linear hiking trail
Closest town: Salem

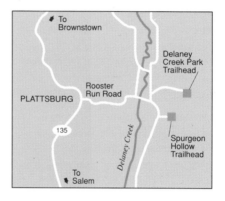

The eastern box turtle is common in most of Indiana's moist, forested areas. Box turtles eat earthworms, slugs, and mushrooms that are poisonous to humans. Males have bright red eyes, while the females' eyes are yellowish-brown.

MARK ROMESSER

FORESTS: MORE THAN JUST TREES

The word forest makes most people think of trees—and rightfully so, because trees are the major component of forests. But the trees are just the beginning—the part you see from the road. A closer look reveals a community of plants and animals that is constantly interacting; growing; and changing.

Trees in the forest grow in layers. The top layer is called the *canopy*, which consists of the leaves and branches of the tallest trees. Leaves in the canopy absorb sunlight and convert it into food for growth and for producing seeds. Beneath the canopy are the smaller trees and shrubs that make up the *understory*. These trees survive in the shade of the canopy. The *forest floor* is where leaves, sticks, and fallen trees decompose, returning nutrients to the soil. The seedlings of tomorrow's forest grow on the forest floor, along with wildflowers, ferns, and other small plants that need very little sunlight.

The forest is constantly changing. As large, old trees fall, they leave holes in the canopy. The sunlight that pours through these holes stimulates smaller trees to grow quickly into the canopy. This, in turn, leaves holes in the understory which are filled by seedlings growing up from the forest floor.

Wildlife play a key role in the life of the forest. Chipmunks and shrews burrow in the forest floor, which aids in the decomposition of fallen leaves. Squirrels bury nuts, serving as a planting service for the next generation of trees. Birds and insects pollinate plants and trees and carry seeds off to grow in new areas.

From the outside, a forest may appear to be just a bunch of trees, but a fascinating association of plants and animals is waiting to be discovered in the deep, shady hallways that lie within. Some people never take the opportunity to look beyond the obvious to find what the forest really is. Such people truly cannot see the forest for the trees.

84 MUSCATATUCK AUTO TOUR

Description: Three-mile auto tour gives a representative look at the Muscatatuck National Wildlife Refuge. Lakes, creeks, flooded timber, and wetlands are found throughout this area of converted agricultural land.

Viewing information: Pick up an auto tour brochure at the visitor center to get the most out of your visit. High probability of viewing wood ducks, Canada geese, and other waterfowl spring through fall. Deer can be viewed year-round. Moderate probability of seeing unusual bird species such as least bitterns, henslow sparrows, and black-crowned night herons in appropriate seasons. The threatened northern copperbelly watersnake is found throughout the refuge. Refuge is open from sunrise to sunset throughout the year.

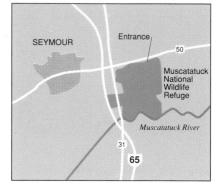

Ownership: U.S. Fish and Wildlife Service (812) 522-4352
Size: 7,724 acres
Closest town: Seymour

85 FALLS OF THE OHIO

Description: When the Ohio River is at low flow levels during the summer and early fall, about 200 acres of 375-million-year-old fossil beds are exposed along the dam on the north bank.

Viewing information: Tidepool-like conditions created by fluctuating water levels are extremely attractive to aquatic bird species. View thousands of gulls, ducks, herons, killdeer, and other birds in the shallow pools and on the rocks. The fossil beds provide a fascinating look at the wildlife of another age. *IF SIREN SOUNDS, LEAVE FOSSIL BEDS IMMEDIATELY. STRONG AND UNPREDICTABLE CURRENTS OCCUR WHEN THE DAM IS OPENED.*

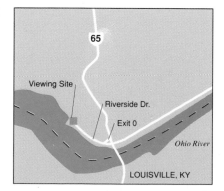

Ownership: Indiana DNR (812) 945-6284
Size: 68 acres, plus 1,404 acres federally-owned
Closest town: Jeffersonville/Clarksville

86 CROSLEY FISH AND WILDLIFE AREA

Description: This area contains wetlands, farm fields, and young forest stands. The Muscatatuck River winds its way through the property, fed by the streams and drainages that run between the moderate to steep slopes that occur throughout the area.

Viewing information: High probability of viewing woodland songbirds, especially in spring. Tree squirrels and raccoons are plentiful and may be viewed throughout the property. Moderate probability of viewing great blue herons, green herons, and several waterfowl species on the river or on any of the small impoundments found in this area. *PUBLIC HUNTING AREA. PLEASE CHECK AT PROPERTY MANAGER'S OFFICE FOR AFFECTED AREAS AND SEASONS.*

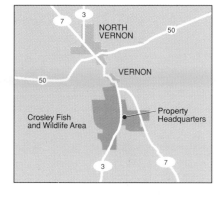

Ownership: Indiana DNR (812) 346-5596
Size: 4,000 acres
Closest town: Vernon/North Vernon

Autumn colors begin to show at Crosley Fish and Wildlife Area.

RICHARD FIELDS/
INDIANA DNR

87 MUSCATATUCK COUNTY PARK

Description: Two hundred sixty acres of steep wooded slopes along the Muscatatuck River. A series of trails traverse the area along ridgetops and river bluffs. Trails running between ridges can be steep with occasional loose stone outcroppings.

Viewing information: High probability of viewing gray squirrels, raccoons, chipmunks, and deer on the woodland trails. Look for turkey vultures along the scenic river bluffs throughout the summer. Developed areas of the park receive heavy use during summer weekends.

Directions: *From downtown North Vernon, take State Road 7 south about one mile to the park entrance. Winding park road leads past several picnic areas to the park office, where trail maps are available. Trails begin near most picnic shelters.*

Ownership: Jennings County Parks Department (812) 346-2953
Size: 260 acres
Closest town: North Vernon/Vernon

Adult Canada geese watch for danger as their goslings explore. Unlike most birds, Canada geese make their fall and spring migrations as family units. This family will remain together until the following breeding season. MARK ROMESSER

Description: Roads and trails wind among majestic wooded gorges, sheer rock cliffs, and plunging waterfalls. Adjacent to the gorges are gently rolling upland areas containing grasses, shrubs, small trees, and other old field vegetation. Several of the trails are extremely steep and rugged. *FALL COLORS AND SPRING WILDFLOWER BLOOMS ARE SPECTACULAR.*

Viewing information: Moderate to high probability of viewing deer from the roads or trails. Hiking trails that run along ridges and canyon walls provide a close look at the birds and other wildlife that live in the very tops of the large, old trees which grow in the valleys below. High probability of viewing turkey vultures, black vultures, and hawks in the canyon on sunny days from spring through fall. These birds glide effortlessly on the warm air currents or thermals that rise up out of the canyon. Hawks are also seen hunting small mammals in the shrubby old field areas around Trail 10.

Ownership: Indiana DNR (812) 265-4135
Size: 1,360 acres
Closest town: Madison

The bluebird's arrival in Indiana is a sure sign that winter is nearly over. The bluebird is also closely related to another harbinger of spring— the robin.
TOM J. ULRICH

89 VERSAILLES STATE PARK

Description: Three meandering creeks flow into scenic Versailles Lake. The lake is surrounded by forests, rocky outcroppings, and shrubby old fields.

Viewing information: High probability of viewing red-tailed hawks, turkey vultures, and black vultures soaring high above the lake and grassy areas. Watch for vultures roosting in the evenings—there may be eighty to 100 birds in a single large tree. Limited probability of seeing red foxes, gray foxes, and coyotes in the forests and fields of this park. Although rarely seen in the act, gray foxes are the only dog-like animals capable of climbing trees. Moderate probability of viewing deer and wild turkeys, especially along park roads in the early morning. Rent a canoe and explore the upper Laughery Creek area for a chance to see herons, songbirds, nonvenomous watersnakes, and turtles. Entry fee required.

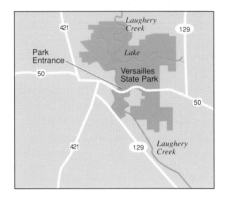

Ownership: Indiana DNR (812) 689-6424
Size: 5,905 acres
Closest town: Versailles

Gray squirrels are very common throughout Indiana, from the deep forest to city parks and neighborhoods. Squirrels can locate buried nuts by smell, even in heavy snow.
JOHN SHAW

Sunset on the salamonie reservoir closes another beautiful day of wildlife watching in Indiana's great outdoors. Plan a trip to see and experience some of this great natural heritage soon. RICHARD FIELDS/INDIANA DNR

POPULAR WILDLIFE VIEWING SPECIES
IN INDIANA–AND WHERE TO FIND THEM

The index below features some of the more interesting, uncommon, or attractive wildlife of Indiana, and some of the best locations for viewing selected species. Many of the animals listed may be viewed at other sites as well.

The Indiana DNR, Division of Fish and Wildlife, receives federal aid from the Sport Fish and Wildlife Restoration programs. Under Title Vi of the 1964 Civil Rights Act, Section 504 of the Rehabilitation Act of 1973, the Age Discrimination Act of 1975, Title IX of the Education Amendments of 1972, the U.S. Government prohibits discrimination on the basis of race, color, national origin, age, sex, or handicap. If you believe that you have been discriminated against in any program, activity, or facility as described above, or if you desire further information please write to:

Division of Fish and Wildlife
402 W. Washington St., Room W273
Indianapolis, IN 46204

Design, typesetting, and other prepress work
by Falcon Press, Helena, Montana

Printed by GTE

Printed in the United States of America

Library of Congress Number 91-05881
ISBN 1-56044-071-6

Printed on Recycled Paper

Wildlife is nearer than you think.
The secret is knowing where and when to look.

From Lake Michigan to the Ohio River, the *Indiana Wildlife Viewing Guide* will lead you to eighty-nine of the state's premier wildlife viewing locations—and better your chances of seeing wildlife once you get there. Included are detailed descriptions of each viewing site, maps and access information, helpful viewing tips, and more than sixty color photos.

This guide was created through the Watchable Wildlife program, a national partnership initiative coordinated by Defenders of Wildlife. Each site was selected by a panel of wildlife experts from the following organizations and government agencies. These groups also made significant technical contributions to the research and development of this guide:

U.S. Forest Service
Indiana Department of Natural Resources
U.S. Fish and Wildlife Service
National Fish and Wildlife Foundation
Indiana Wildlife Federation
Defenders of Wildlife
GTE
Northern Indiana Public Service Company
PSI Energy
Indiana Department of Transportation
Indiana Department of Commerce,
   Division of Tourism and Marketing
   Development
South Bend Audubon Society

Amos Butler Chapter, The Audubon Society
Indiana Chapter, The Wildlife Society
Association of Indiana Convention and Visitors
   Bureaus
National Park Service
Indiana Bowhunters Association
The Nature Conservancy

FALCON PRESS®

ISBN 1-56044-071-6 $5.95